The Fulham

Rugby League tackle.

By Harold Genders

London League Publications Ltd

The Fulham Dream
Rugby League tackles London

Front cover photo: Iain MacCorquodale kicking a goal at Fulham
Back cover photo: Fulham team at start of 1980-1981 season. Included in the group are Jack Myerscough (Rugby League Chairman), David Oxley (Rugby League General Secretary) and David Howes (Rugby League Public Relations Officer)

A CIP catalogue record for this book is available from the British Library.

First published in Great Britain in August 2000 by:
London League Publications Ltd.
P.O. Box 10441, London E14 0SB

ISBN: 0-9526064-9-6

Cover design by: Stephen McCarthy Graphic Design
                          46, Clarence Road, London N15 5BB
Layout by: Peter Lush
Printed and bound by: Catford Print Centre, PO Box 563, Catford,
                          London SE6 4PY

This book is dedicated to my wife Shirley and to the players and supporters of Fulham RLFC. Thank you for your support in establishing Rugby League in London.

Foreword

The four years I spent as Fulham's player/coach were the best years of my life. Harold Genders phoned me in June 1980 and asked if I was interested in joining Fulham. "I don't know anything about soccer" was my light-hearted response. But then he outlined his plans for a Rugby League club at Fulham and explained his vision to me. I discussed it with my wife Brenda and we agreed it would be a good move for me. It was hard for me to leave Widnes, my home town club, where I had enjoyed 12 successful years, but the move to Fulham was a new challenge and gave me the chance to break into coaching.

Harold managed to persuade the Widnes directors to sell me, and then we worked together building the team. We would discuss the players we wanted and then Harold would do the wheeling and dealing to sign them. He had a good eye for players and I respected his judgement.

We completed signing the players just before the Wigan match. One of our young players, Tony Kinsey, was getting married the day before we played Wigan. He couldn't play in the match, but he bought his new wife to watch the occasion.

I dealt with all the training and team selection. Harold never pressurised me about team selection and was always interested in our training. He would come for a drink with the players after training. He is very knowledgeable about Rugby League and is a genuine enthusiast for the sport. He loved being involved with the players.

Harold had a vision for how Fulham should develop. But after the first season we were never given enough funding to build the team to compete at the top level. That was why Harold left the club in September 1983.

The match after Harold resigned, we were playing Hull at Craven Cottage. Hull then was one of the top teams. The players' heads were down because of Harold leaving. I said to them before the game: "let's win this one for the boss". We tore into Hull in the first half and hung on for an unexpected victory. But after that the writing was on the wall for Rugby League at Craven Cottage and I left the club in June 1984 to become coach of Warrington.

I didn't know Harold well before I joined Fulham, only on a social level when he was a director of Warrington. But we became the best of friends during our time together at Fulham, and still are.

I am very pleased that Harold's book about his time at Fulham is being published. It recalls the good times we spent building Rugby League in London.

Reg Bowden

Harold Genders (on left) in the dugout at Craven Cottage
(Photo courtesy Harold Genders)

Introduction

London League Publications Ltd is delighted to be able to publish this book, telling the inside story of how Fulham RLFC was set up and how promotion was won in the club's memorable first season.

There was great excitement at the birth of Rugby League at Fulham. Back in 1980 professional Rugby League was confined to the game's heartlands in the north of England. There had not been a new entrant to the League since 1954. The game was played in the south by a few amateur clubs, but was absent from most Londoners' sporting awareness, apart from television coverage of the Challenge Cup on BBC television's *Grandstand*.

Since 1980 there have been various attempts to develop the game in new areas. Some have been successful, especially outside the professional ranks. Amongst students, in the summer Conference and in the armed forces the game has grown in new parts of the country and society. However, attempts to develop professional clubs outside the heartlands have been less successful, usually because of inadequate funding. It is ironic that as this year marks the 20th anniversary of the founding of Fulham RLFC, the club, now the London Broncos, is again the only professional one in Britain outside the north of England.

Harold Genders's idea of a club in London was years ahead of its time. The original concept of Super League 15 years later was of big city clubs winning new audiences to the game, a concept now seemingly abandoned. Harold had already created one. Yet, satellite television has given Rugby League an enormous opportunity to reach new audiences. Whether the game can take this chance is another matter.

If the directors at Fulham provided funds to build a successful team in the top flight, Harold's dream of a top class Rugby League club in London could have been fully realised. As it was, Fulham never developed the potential shown in the first season. Instead, they went up and down between the First and Second Divisions before the directors abandoned their experiment in Rugby League in 1984. The club then left Craven Cottage to rebuild under new owners, Roy and Barbara Close.

We hope that readers enjoy this book. It is the story of an important part of Rugby League's rich history and part of the fascinating history of Rugby League in London.

Peter Lush and Dave Farrar
July 2000

About the author

Harold Genders joined Rochdale Hornets in 1949 as a nineteen year old scrum-half. He was then an apprentice joiner and studying part-time for the Higher National Certificate and City and Guilds in construction at Warrington Technical College.

His studies allowed him to defer his compulsory national service until he was 21. He then spent two years in the RAF, based at Stoke Heath. He continued to play for Rochdale at weekends, but also has some fond memories of playing Rugby Union in the RAF. He was captain-coach of the RAF Stoke Heath team and played for Maintenance Command and the Combined Services.

When he left the RAF he played Rugby League for Widnes and Blackpool Borough before retiring at the end of the 1957-1958 season to concentrate on developing his career in the construction industry.

He joined Leonard Fairclough Ltd in 1959. The company is now known as AMEC plc and is one of Britain's largest construction firms. He was promoted 18 times and became managing director of Fairclough Civil Engineering. He retired in 1997.

He became involved with Warrington RLFC in the mid 1970s when the late Sir Oswald Davies, AMEC's chairman, bought the club. Harold founded the Primrose Club at Warrington to help raise funds for the club, and then became a director, mainly working on player recruitment.

He left Warrington in 1980 to become managing director of the newly formed Fulham RLFC and stayed at Fulham until September 1983. In 1988, he became managing director at Swinton RLFC, again playing a major role in player recruitment which saw the team reach the Divisional Premiership final. He left Swinton in 1989, frustrated by financial problems at the club.

He still takes an interest in Rugby League, although he finds the game very different today from the one he grew up with. He other main sporting interest is cricket and he is a member of Lancashire CCC. He lives in Glazebury (near Warrington) with his wife, Shirley.

The rest of the team

Colin Gibson was Harold's original co-author when the first version of this book was written in the early 1980s. He also wrote a regular column in the club's programme from 1980 to 1984. He was appointed southern Rugby League corespondent of the *Daily Telegraph* when Fulham was founded because he was the only northerner in the paper's London office. He always had a love of Rugby League having been born and bred in Manchester and was thrilled to be in at the birth of a special team.

He remained the correspondent until September 1982 when he was appointed as a football writer. He kept close ties with Fulham until he moved to the *Daily Mail* in December 1984. Since then he became chief sports reporter of the *Daily Telegraph* in 1986 and covered the football European Championships and World Cups as well as Commonwealth Games and every Olympic Games since 1984. In June 1993 he was appointed Sports Editor of the *Sunday Telegraph* and in march 1999 was named British Sports Journalist of the year by the Sports Council. In October 1999 he moved to Sydney to take up the post of Assistant Editor (Sports) with *The Australian* newspaper. His main task has been preparing the paper for the Sydney Olympic Games but he also remains closely in touch with the NRL, the strongest Rugby League competition in the world. He did not play any part in the updating and final editing of the book.

Peter Lush worked with Harold to revise the book and carry out further editing and research. He was introduced to Rugby League at Fulham in 1980 and has followed the game every since. With Dave Farrar he was co-author of *Touch and Go - A History of Rugby League in London* and co-editor of *From Fulham to Wembley - 20 Years of Rugby League in London.*

Dave Farrar carried out much of the research for the appendices for the book and assisted with the editing. He was brought up on Rugby League in Salford, before moving to London in 1980. By a happy coincidence Fulham RLFC started six months later and he was able to continue watching the game. He has also co-written or co-edited five books on the sport.

Our thanks also to:
Michael O'Hare for his advice and skills in sub-editing.
Ken Coton for providing photos.
Denise Clarke for typing the original manuscript

Rugby League in 1980

Rugby League in 1980 was in some ways a very different game from the one we know today. The scoring gave three points for a try instead of four as it is today.

Scrums were also very different from today, when the team feeding the scrum is virtually certain to keep possession. The ball had to be fed into the tunnel between the two packs, where the hookers would strike for it. This made the position of hooker far more specialist and important than it is today, as a poor hooker could mean a team being starved of possession, as they would lose the ball at the scrums.

Each team was only allowed two substitutes. A player who was replaced by a substitute could act as a substitute themselves, but only once. Substitutions played a far smaller role in the game's tactics than they do today.

The professional league structure in 1980 had two divisions, with the bottom four teams in the First Division being relegated to the Second Division each season, and the top four teams from the Second Division being promoted. There was quite a wide gap in standards between the two divisions and often teams were promoted one season and relegated the next. They became known as "yo-yo" teams.

Virtually all the players were part-time and worked during the day. They would train two or three evenings a week.

Rugby Union in 1980 was still officially an "amateur" game. For a Rugby Union player to turn professional in Rugby League was a major decision, as they would then be banned from playing Rugby Union again.

About this book

The original draft of this book was written in the early 1980s, when Harold was Managing Director at Fulham. We have kept editing to a minimum, except where it was necessary to add points of clarification so that the book could be understood by readers who have only recently become interested in Rugby League. The final chapter was written this year to round off the story. The appendices were written by Peter Lush and Dave Farrar.

Contents

Chapter 1: The dream

Rugby League is not a sport which is normally associated with dreams or dreamers. Like the people who play it, Rugby League is a down-to-earth, no frills, sport. Romantics in the sport are as difficult to find as a prima donna in the mud and gore of Doncaster on a wind blown, rain-lashed, winter Sunday afternoon. But, just once, I allowed myself and Rugby League one dream and, as a result, Fulham Rugby League Club was born in 1980 and with it the fairytale first season that came to an end just 12 months later.

On the way, my men had battled from Dewsbury's Crown Flatt to Doncaster's Tattersfield to Huddersfield's Fartown. Finally, in the back streets of Rochdale at their old home stadium, the Athletic Grounds, the triumph was complete.

The carnival replaced the dream. The final night celebration was staged at Craven Cottage on Friday, 1 May 1981, on Challenge Cup Final eve. First Division Champions Bradford Northern were the sacrificial lambs that evening and 11,926 people came to see the feast.

In a year the club had come a tremendous distance. Bradford were beaten 20-8, with Dave Allen scoring four tries and, on an evening like that, it would have been impossible for any side to have beaten Fulham, backed by the emotional charge of their supporters.

The achievements were a success for Rugby League in a wider context. Fulham had spread the gospel to the south of England and, most importantly, had done it - in the short term - successfully .

One Rugby League writer called this time the "Age of the game" - and it was Fulham who had brought public interest back to the game and for Rugby League set off an express.

In the mid-1970s, Rugby League was dying a slow and painful death and then suddenly, after the arrival of Fulham, for two or three seasons, it became the boom sport in Britain. New clubs, amateur and professional opened all over the country and it was mainly because of Fulham's venture. They captured the imagination of the British sporting public as no other Rugby League side until that time had ever done. Until Fulham came into existence, in modern times the idea of

1

leaving the traditional Rugby League homelands of the northern industrial towns was unthinkable. Of course, those times for Rugby league were very different from today. The players were part-time, and the game was far less commercial than today. There was far less television coverage and no satellite television with the amount of matches shown nationally by SKY today. There was far less national awareness of Rugby League, with the game's presence in the south being restricted to a few amateur clubs.

Therefore, it was not surprising that many people thought it would be a disaster to start a new club outside the sport's traditional areas. The experiments in South Wales, London and the north east in the 1930s and 1940s had failed. The last new side, Blackpool Borough, was in financial problems - why should Fulham succeed?

They did though and despite the problems that relegation brought the following season, they showed the character and strength to bounce back and take the Second Division title in their third season.

Fulham's magnificent gamble paid off and clubs such as Cardiff, Carlisle and Kent Invicta, based in Maidstone, took off while other sides at Bolton, Notts County, Portsmouth, Crystal Palace, Reading, both Bristol clubs and Hearts and Rangers in Scotland looked hard at the prospect - all because of Fulham. Carlisle lasted until the 1990s before merging with Barrow. Cardiff and Kent Invicta sadly did not last the course, both clubs needed more investment to succeed.

The amateur side of the game has also prospered in places such as Hemel Hempstead, Fulham and Ealing in the south and Sunderland in the north. Schools Rugby League flourished and the first University game between Oxford and Cambridge took place at Craven Cottage on Sunday 26 April, 1981 in what is proving to be one of the biggest steps forward Rugby League has ever made. If there had not been a Fulham, it is unlikely there would have been a Carlisle, a Cardiff or much of the development since outside the heartlands, in areas such as the new summer Conference League, the colleges and universities and the armed forces.

Jack Bentley wrote in the *Daily Express* - "As far away as Sydney, where Rugby League is the king and soccer is well down the popularity stakes, the first question that greeted the English aficionados of the game was: 'How are Fulham doing?'"

The great thing for the game was that Fulham did everything correctly and I am pleased to have had the privilege of playing a major part in the venture. It was a team that broke down the old frontiers of the game; a side that went out and attracted new spectators to the sport. It was an inspired move, possibly successful ... perhaps undoubtedly so. Look back at that first historic season. Fulham helped set record gates wherever they played. They rekindled interest in the sport. Once again, Rugby League was back in the headlines. In the John Player Trophy, they set a competition record with their first round gate against Leeds - only beaten that season by the attendance in the final.

In the Second Division, gates were up by an incredible 39.2% and as David Oxley, the Secretary of the Rugby League said, most of the increase was due to Fulham. In fact, Fulham added 85,000 fans to the Second Division and seven clubs increased their gates on the previous year, because of the Fulham supporters and interest the team attracted. I also understand that Whitehaven had their best League attendance for some 20 years for Fulham's visit. Fulham finished with an average attendance of 6,096 in league games with an overall average attendance, including cup ties, of 7,150. The average league attendances were 4,091 bigger than the overall Second Division clubs' average figure. In the Challenge Cup, the 15,013 spectators at the Wakefield game on 15 February, 1981 at Craven Cottage was the third highest domestic gate in the game, excluding the Challenge Cup Final at Wembley.

In the first three seasons, Fulham won awards galore, were promoted twice and all this was on a shoestring budget and squad of, at times, as few as 15 fit players.

When Bradford Northern left Craven Cottage after their side's defeat they knew they had been in on something really big. "You have a great side," said their Chairman, Jack Bates, after the game. Not a bad start for a team which eight months before the eve of Wembley match, did not exist.

3

Fulham versus Bradford Northern 1 May 1981

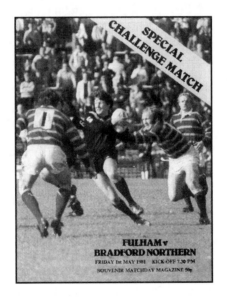

Chapter 2: Joining the League

Ironically, it was at Wembley where the dream began. I was staying at Quaglino's, a London hotel where years before, Amy Johnson had stayed when planning her historic flight across the Atlantic. Someone who had fulfilled her dream. Two years before the big night against Bradford Northern, I sat in my room searching through the southern editions of the national and local newspapers, desperately looking for a reference to the Widnes versus Wakefield Trinity 1979 Challenge Cup Final the next day.

None was to be found. On the Sunday after the game, watched by 96,000 people, all that could be found was the result. The miserly result. This was Rugby League's biggest day and all it merited - in southern eyes - was a single line score.

Something, I thought, must be done to spread the gospel, but how? The only possibility could be the creation of a Rugby League club in the south. A southern outpost. But where?

On the Monday, I obtained a map of England and searched for the right venue. After much deliberation, I decided there were two alternatives, Hereford United or Fulham.

Hereford, newly voted into the Football League, had returned swiftly to the Fourth (now Third) Division after an encouraging start to their League career. Hereford itself was in an ideal position. Close to the Welsh borders, close to the mass of population in the Midlands, yet linked with the old established areas of Rugby League by the M5 and M6 motorways.

Relegation for any soccer club is a costly matter. Gates tumble, advertising revenue drops and players leave. Rugby League could be the medicine the bank balances desperately needed.

Fulham, once proud FA Cup Finalists and First Division material were also faltering. After a dreadful season, they had been relegated to the Third (now Second) Division. Their Chairman, the late Ernie Clay, a man who was prepared to take risks, fascinated me.

Ernie Clay was not frightened to venture into the unknown. He had signed former England captain Bobby Moore, the controversial

George Best and Rodney Marsh and had shown the risks he was prepared to take.

London, in my opinion, is the greatest city in the world and to have a Rugby League side there would be the greatest boost the sport had ever had. The site at Craven Cottage was also ideal.

Within a mile of the ground is Earls Court, where many Australians and New Zealanders live. Both codes of rugby and Rugby League, in particular, is very popular in these two countries so the question was: would they support us? In any event, London, with around eight million people was potentially the greatest source of support for a new Rugby League club.

After a lot of deliberation, I decided.... Fulham was my target. The problem was how could the target be achieved. It took a year, until 1980, before my opportunity presented itself.

Again, it was Challenge Cup Final week at Wembley. I rang up Mr Clay's secretary on the pretence I had heard, on the Rugby League grapevine, that he was looking for two tickets for the Wembley match between Hull and Hull Kingston Rovers. I had two tickets to spare because two of my guests were unable to make the trip, due to illness. Of course, he had never wanted any tickets.

Unfortunately, he was ill, but his secretary passed on the message and the seed was sown. I sat back and waited for the Fulham chairman to ring back, as I knew he would, if the newspaper reports about him were correct. He would be curious. Sure enough, later that week, the phone rang and Rugby League at Fulham was on the way.

All the negotiations had to be carried out in secret because I was still a director at First Division Warrington Rugby League club. It was not a case of being a traitor to the Warrington cause - the club were, and still are, very close to my heart - but this was a chance to further the cause of Rugby League. In a choice between club and sport, the sport came first.

So secret were my talks that Ernie Clay was later to refer to me, on television, as the "mole". Malcolm MacDonald, Fulham's commercial manager and former England international footballer, watching television with me joked: "how does it feel to be called a mole?"

6

When that first call did come through it was Brian Dalton, Fulham's financial director, who was on the line. "What is it all about?" was his question. I refused to discuss the matter over the telephone, so he suggested that we should meet at the Saxon Hotel, just outside Huddersfield.

That meeting took place on 6 May 1980. Dalton brought Gregory Clay, Ernie's son, with him and I shocked them both by suggesting that Fulham should sell their soccer team and take up Rugby League full-time.

"I thought you told us that you weren't mad," said Dalton. The other alternative, I told him, was to play Rugby League at Craven Cottage every other week. That caught their interest and after I outlined the advantages of playing rugby, as a back-up to soccer, they left to put the scheme to Ernie Clay.

I was a little concerned that Ernie was not present at the meeting but Dalton, who was going on holiday to Hawaii, assured me that he would contact me again on his return.

The omens were not good. Both Bobby Campbell, the club's team manager and Ted Drake, a director and former England and Arsenal footballer, were dead set against the scheme.

On 28 May, I was invited down to Craven Cottage for the first time to meet the board. When I arrived in London, I found that Ernie Clay was not present again.

Dalton said, rightly, that if Ernie, a domineering character had been at the meeting, the board would be inhibited and would go along with his opinion, whether they agreed or not.

There was quite an impressive turnout for the meeting; Bobby Campbell, Malcolm MacDonald and Ted Drake were joined by Brian Dalton and myself.

Bobby Campbell complained that the pitch would be ruined and suggested that Fulham's football gates could improve, even though they had been relegated the previous season. His argument was based on the club doing well in the Third Division. Campbell was firing a lot of bullets at the scheme, but many proved to be blanks.

Ted Drake was in a similar frame of mind. A traditional soccer

7

man through and through, he claimed that soccer was the only game that should be played at Craven Cottage. Again, his arguments did not seem to carry weight.

The two men who spoke out in favour of the plan were, of course, Brian Dalton but, surprisingly, Malcolm MacDonald. I will be eternally grateful for the help that they gave. Malcolm's only worry was "Could we buy a team in time?" I told him that it could be done without any problems and both Brian and Malcolm gave the "thumbs-up" to the dream.

So, against a background of mixed feelings about the idea, we drove to Ernie Clay's home in Surrey. Any worries I had were dispelled as soon as I arrived.

A champagne lunch - a kind of celebration - was laid on and it was then that I realised that no matter what the board thought of the idea, Ernie was completely behind it. Nothing was going to stop him having Rugby League.

In fact, if Ernie set his mind on something, nothing could stop him and this attitude was to prove very valuable in the battles we fought later. His only question was: "What are our prospects?"

"We will be promoted in the first year," I replied. The man never questioned me. "Get on and do it," was his instruction.

We shook hands on the deal and that was that. There were no long drawn out board meetings. Ernie had decided that he wanted Rugby League at Craven Cottage and he was determined to get it. Later, during the birth of the club, he was to prove a vigorous and determined fighter in keeping the scheme alive.

If I thought that the hard work had been done, I had a shock coming to me. We were now facing the hardest part of all. The Rugby League had to be persuaded to change its rules to even allow Fulham's application to be considered, as we had missed the date for new clubs to apply for the forthcoming season.

If that was not enough, I then - along with the help of Ernie Clay and Brian Dalton - had to persuade the 30 Rugby Football League member clubs to accept a totally new club for the first time in almost 30 years. It was sink or swim for Rugby League at Fulham and I was determined we would swim.

On 11 June, I invited Jack Myerscough, then chairman of the Rugby League, and David Oxley, the Rugby League secretary, to Craven Cottage. I met them on the Leeds to London train along with Brian Dalton, and when we arrived at Kings Cross, I still felt I had a lot to do to persuade them the project was worthwhile. At that time, a team in London was an extraordinary idea for Rugby League. There had been no expansion outside the north of England for years. They were naturally cautious.

Then came the piece of luck that everyone needs. Outside King's Cross, I found my secret weapon... a London taxi driver. As he drove across Central London, the driver was quietly and discreetly quizzed by David Oxley about Rugby League. To my delight, the driver went into raptures. "Best thing that could ever 'appen at the Cottage. Better than that soccer. Not the violence, is there? Me and the missus would be down there every fortnight cheering the side on. Marvellous, just bloody marvellous."

I just sat back and let the club's unofficial spokesman do the talking. Out of all the taxi drivers in London - and there are thousands - we had found a Rugby League fanatic. I could not believe my luck.

Later, someone jokingly suggested that he had been sent by Ernie Clay, but nothing could have been further from the truth.

As we approached Craven Cottage, Jack Myerscough, fearing a set-up job, asked the taxi driver who he thought his passengers were. He knew we had travelled down on the Leeds train and, quick as a flash, told him: "You're that Manny Cousins (the Leeds United FC chairman) and you've come down to buy one of their football players. Don't know what you see in any of them myself."

With that, Jack, a great character, laughed and told him we were actually connected with Rugby League. I am not claiming that the taxi driver actually convinced Oxley and Myerscough that Fulham's venture would be a success, but it did no harm.

After a tour around the Craven Cottage stadium, we returned to King's Cross and despite the effects of the taxi driver and the impressive ground, I was not sure our guests were in favour.

My worst thoughts were realised on our trip back north when David Oxley agreed that the facilities were marvellous but suggested we should wait a season. Under the Rugby League's rules, we had missed the chance for new clubs to join for the forthcoming season and would now need a change of rules and a special meeting to even have our scheme put before the clubs.

"Wait another year," said Oxley. But I did not accept that. "If I wait another year, that will only give me three weeks to a month more time than I have now. I cannot sign anyone before we've been voted into the League," I said. We would face the same problem a year on - we could not sign players if we were not sure of being in the League.

"Nobody in their right minds would join a side that was not even in the League and had no matches to play," I said. I think that clinched it.

Myerscough swung his considerable influence behind us. Oxley saw the sense of it and suddenly, from being years away from acceptance, we were now only days away.

Now all that was needed to be done was to change the Rugby League's rules. In itself, this was no easy task, but with the backing of powerful men like Myerscough and Oxley, I was convinced that this could be done. We needed a two-thirds majority of the League's 30 clubs and the special meeting was convened before the Rugby League's Annual General Meeting at Harrogate which was to be held on Friday 27 June 1980.

This was the moment of truth. We held a "council of war" over lunch the day before the meeting at the Queen's Hotel, Leeds, to discuss our strategy. Obviously, I would not be able to attend the meeting to put forward Fulham's case, because my cover would be blown - I was still a Warrington director and so Ernie Clay had to be primed for this vital last round.

At the lunch were Oxley, Myerscough, Ernie Clay, Eddie Waring, the famous Rugby League television commentator, and myself. We were convinced that the clubs would approve our plan. The advantages, and our expertise, far outweighed the problems of travel and time. We knew it could be done, all that was left was to persuade the clubs.

10

I travelled back to my home in Glazebury and waited for the outcome. My resignation as a director of Warrington was already written, that was how confident I was. But, even so, it was still a long wait. So many things could have gone wrong. But, in fact, everything went very smoothly.

The special meeting first considered whether or not to waive the red tape and consider Fulham's application. When the vote was taken, it was a unanimous decision to consider the scheme.

It followed that the clubs would accept Fulham. As it happened, they did, but surprisingly, not unanimously. Instead, they voted 26 for, with three abstentions, none against. They were Bradford Northern, Rochdale Hornets and Halifax, with Huyton not having attended. History had been made at the Majestic Hotel, Harrogate. Fulham were in the Slalom Lager Second Division.

My wife, Shirley, and I were travelling that evening to Liverpool. We were going on a trip along the Mersey, on the famous Liverpool ferry, the Royal Iris, with Keith Pennington, one of my contract managers from work. We heard the 6pm news on the car radio which confirmed that Fulham had been accepted as members of the Rugby Football League.

It was a time for celebration but I made Keith stop the car, because there was one important task still to be performed. I remember it well. It was in Billinge, a small town near St. Helens, that I finally posted my resignation as a director to Warrington RLFC. It was a jubilant moment, yet still sad.

I had been brought up in Warrington. I had watched Warrington RLFC as a lad and had even as a played Rugby League for the town side. I had been on the board there since 1975 and had helped in the signings of players such as Billy Benyon, who went on to become the club's coach, Ken Kelly, the captain, and many others.

They had a fine side and were a fine club, but the move, no matter how much a wrench, had to be made. Progress in the sport came before an individual club.

One of the major surprises was that the whole operation was kept so secret. Rugby League is not a sport known for its secrecy. Within

11

minutes of a man being signed, or a player wanting a move, everybody knows. This time, it appears, everyone remained tight-lipped and, in fact, David Oxley has referred to the whole thing as one of the best kept secrets the sport has ever had.

In secrecy, there was nothing sinister. I did not want to burn all my boats. If Fulham had not gained entry into the League, I would still have wanted to continue at Warrington. My resignation was received generously by Warrington. A few weeks later, I received a letter thanking me for my work for the club and I was also mentioned in the annual report in the usual way.

There was no ill feeling and I was glad, because I had the greatest regard for the Warrington chairman Mr Brian Pitchford, director Tony Bingham, the players and staff.

Fulham voted into the Rugby League

One newspaper's response to the League's decision

At the start of July, Malcolm MacDonald and Brian Dalton emerged into the full glare of the publicity machine. They travelled to Leeds for further discussions with the Rugby League and to meet the press. Malcolm was interviewed on Yorkshire Television and had his picture taken running past David Oxley, with a rugby ball. The whole impact of the situation began to sink in. Malcolm must have been the first Fulham person, other than myself, to actually touch a rugby ball.

I met Malcolm and Brian and had a meal with them that evening at Brian's home, as we were to journey south for a board meeting. As we were meandering along the M1 motorway, I suddenly burst out laughing. Malcolm and Brian were obviously nonplussed. "What's the matter?" they said. I said: "it seems like a joke. We are the only team in the Rugby League without a jersey, a ball, a set of posts, a match or any players." Joke it may have been, but we soon sorted the whole thing out. Within days, I plunged into the transfer market. Fulham was on its way and I was aware of the fact that history was being made.

Chapter 3: Players

"For Christ's sake, Harold, don't sign any more players and the seven of us will share the winning money," said former Great Britain star Tony Karalius after I had signed him from Wigan. That was how confident he was that Fulham would do well in the Second Division.

Within nine days of gaining entry into the Rugby League, I had managed to sign seven top-class players, albeit that one or two were a bit long in the tooth. We were on our way but it had not been easy.

We had to be successful. There was no doubt that Fulham people (who were not indoctrinated in the game) would not pay hard-earned cash to come and see a side lose each week in the Second Division. So, with my initial £100,000 from Fulham, I set out to build a side which I recognised did not only have to win matches but must also gain promotion. Despite Karalius's optimism, £100,000 for 15 players resulted in each player costing approximately £6,500 (providing I only bought 15 players) and at that price, there was little chance of that standard of player winning many games. In any event, I set out to do the best I could with limited financial resources and a lot of hope.

So, in the early days, it was a question of plunging into the bargain basement, not necessarily for free-transfer players but for experienced men with the big match temperament.

The side also needed balance. A team of old stagers would have possibly carried us through a season but at the end of it, I would have needed to splash out again on another team. So the delicate balance between youth and experience was vitally important. I have always believed that a good side consisted of a good pack and that big forwards were better than small ones and fast backs were better than slow ones.

During a fortnight's holiday, I set about the massive task of building the side. Some holiday! In between renovating a room at my home, I was on the telephone to a considerable number of chairmen and Rugby League players. In the end, I was talking to so many people I became completely confused. It must be appreciated that when you speak to anyone in regard to buying one of their players, there is a certain amount of bargaining that takes place. Very rarely, if at all, are figures quoted and accepted at the first time of asking and, when you are buying a whole team, there are negotiations with many chairmen taking place at once. In the end, with so much going on, I was getting my deals mixed up. However, I finally managed to buy the right players from the right clubs at the right price.

My first move, however, was back to Wilderspool. During my time as a director at Warrington, I had helped with the signings of Billy Benyon, John Dalgreen (later to join me at Fulham), Neil Courtney and Ken Kelly and had spoken to many Welsh Rugby Union players as well as New Zealand All Blacks.

I knew the good players and the prices I could afford so when Warrington offered Roy Lester a free-transfer, I moved in. He fitted the identikit picture of a forward. He was a well-built, fast player who could take tackles and I knew that he was of First Division standard. I decided to have tentative talks and arranged to meet him on 22 June 1980 - even before Fulham were voted into the League - in the hope that he would not sign for anyone else.

I was lucky and although he was talking to Second Division strugglers Huddersfield, he had not actually agreed to join them. He arrived, with his wife, at my home and I broke the news to him. The astonishment was very apparent. He nearly fell off the chair, but the challenge appealed to him and even though Huddersfield were also chasing him, he decided to make history and become Fulham's first signing. We were on our way.

I attempted to contact Workington, then in the First Division, with regard to Iain MacCorquodale, a proven goal-kicker, who was on the transfer list at £8,000. It should be appreciated that in every game, penalties are awarded and goal-kickers win matches. One of the reasons I had always supported Steve Hesford's selection at Warrington is because I understood that fact. He was a good full-back and strong player worthy of his place anyway, but his goal-kicking was a bonus. Strangely enough, while trying to contact Iain, I received a telephone call from him at home and Iain expressed his interest in Fulham. In many ways it was very fortunate because two of the hardest positions to fill in any team are hooker and goal-kicker. Now I had filled one of those positions. Here was a man with many goals to his credit wishing to join us who would carry out the goal-kicking role.

I rang Denis Pattison at Workington and then, after much negotiation, we finally agreed £6,000 for Iain was acceptable. At this stage, I could only agree terms due to the fact I did not have the players' contract forms. However, I did have agreement with two players and, once again, Huddersfield, who had also been interested in Iain, were pipped at the post.

The problem of not having forms nearly worked against my third signing. I'd had initial talks with centre Derek Noonan and his club, First Division giants St Helens, on 28 June and agreed a £4,000 fee. Thinking that Derek was "in the bag" I moved on to other players and didn't contact him again until 3 July, only to find that he had changed his mind. Derek, a successful English international, was important to my plan. He would give us experience, his defence in the centre position was second to none and I was stunned when he revealed he was having second thoughts. I knew his wife was expecting a baby and he had thought it over and decided that weekends away in London would not be very fair to her. I also understood another club were interested. Of course, the players were to continue living and training in the north, as they were part-time Rugby League professionals and would not move to London, but would spend weekends in London for home games. Our training was at the Golborne Sports Club, a couple of miles from my home in Leigh.

I was now in an unfortunate position. I had told the press that Noonan was a Fulham player, and now he was thinking of backing out. Luckily, after about an hour's persuasion, he agreed that he would, in fact, sign and come to Craven Cottage. I was relieved and immediately finalised the players' agreements and promised myself that I would never find myself in that position again. Registration was very important to us.

Publicity was also very important. Ernie Clay always said, there is no bad publicity (I disagree as I considered our publicity had to be co-ordinated carefully because of the number of the transfer deals we

15

were doing). The success of Fulham depended upon enough people coming to watch us and we required a minimum of 3,500 to 4,000 each home game. That estimate proved to be insufficient. When you were living and training more than 200 miles away from your home ground, it was easy to misjudge the costs involved. A more realistic gate of 5,000 to 5,500 proved to be necessary.

I decided to use as much publicity as possible and to do that, I needed to keep the Fulham name in the paper day by day, week by week. My ploy in that respect was to release the names of the players I had signed at the rate of one a day wherever possible, even though some were already signed. This had the effect of keeping prices down in the negotiations because had the other clubs realised I had signed so many First Division standard players so soon, the prices would undoubtedly have risen.

But, in not releasing the name of my next signing, John Risman, the experienced Blackpool player, he thought that I was not going to bring him to Craven Cottage. John made the original approach and I agreed over the telephone to sign him but with the lack of publicity, he thought he had been overlooked. Luckily, when he called me, a little worriedly, the following week, I was able to explain and reassure him.

In between John and Derek, I made my most important signing. It was vital, with only £100,000 to spend, that I had a player/coach. So I went through the Rugby League player registrations searching for the right man. I thought of players such as David Topliss of First Division Wakefield, the St Helens pair, Roy Mathias and George Nicholls, together with Widnes's favourite son, Reg Bowden, and many others.

The obvious first choice was Bowden. He had the perfect pedigree. He had played under top coaches Vince Karalius, Frank Myler and Doug Laughton; with Alex Murphy, Billy Benyon and Peter Fox some of the best coaches in the world. Something must have rubbed off. He had the big match experience, but his enthusiasm had not been diluted by the sweet taste of success. He had a great personality, something that would be so important when dealing with the press and, more importantly, the club's new spectators.

We wanted people to come through the turnstiles and it was

important that we had a person who was capable of communicating, someone the people could identify with. There was no contest - it had to be Bowden.

The big problem now would be persuading the successful First Division Widnes club to release him. I approached them on three occasions and their chairman, the late Jack Woodward asked me, through Reg Bowden, to attend a meeting with their committee.

On Tuesday evening, 1 July, I turned up at their Naughton Park ground prepared to meet the committee - 12 just men. It was obvious that several were determined not to part with him. Many were torn between not wanting to lose him and not wanting to stand in his way. I was confident I could persuade them with the help of a £25,000 cheque. I knew Bowden wanted to move to Fulham. This was his big chance to become a full-time player/coach.

Widnes finally gave way. The player they had signed as an 18-year-old in 1968 for £250 was leaving for £25,000 - a quarter of the cash I had available. Keith Macklin of ITV later described it as the perfect choice whilst Jack McNamara of the *Manchester Evening News*, said signing Bowden was a touch of genius. Genius or not, it certainly gave the whole venture a touch of credibility. People who had dismissed us as a joke were now made to sit up and think. The record transfer fee at the time in Rugby League was £38,000 paid by Hull KR for Len Casey.

The signing of Reg - who I consider, along with Parry Gordon of Warrington, desperately unlucky not to play for Great Britain - also helped us to sign quality players such as Mal Aspey, David Eckersley, David Allen from Widnes and John Wood from Wigan, who had recently retired at 24 years of age.

After the meeting, Reg and I had a drink and we were to turn our sights now to the rest of the team. But with only five players on the books, I had filled three of the four crucial positions.

Bowden was scrum-half and player/coach with MacCorquodale as goal-kicker. My next priority was to find a hooker and in Rugby League there are many average hookers, some good but very few great ones. Unlike the game now, in those days, when the scrum-half fed the

17

ball into the tunnel for the hookers to fight for, a quality ball-winner was essential.

I was lucky, Tony Karalius was thinking of retiring. A World Cup player in 1972 and now 33 years old, I knew he had the necessary experience and ability to give Fulham one good season which would gain us promotion to the First Division. I approached Wigan and with their chairman on holiday, I dealt with the late Sumner Baxendale. I agreed a fee of £2,500, rather expensive, but I needed a hooker I could rely on. I believe this was the last negotiation on a player that Sumner handled before retiring as a director of the Wigan club.

Having agreed terms with Wigan, five minutes persuasion was all it took to convince Tony. He promised me that he would play for a season and he stood by his word. His real class shone in the matches against the top sides, Leeds, Wakefield and Bradford. In those games he showed that class players never lose their touch. The legs may be a little slower, but the brain works just as fast.

Tony proved to be the ideal club captain and with seven players on the books, the crucial positions had been filled. Now it was a case of buying the rest of the side.

Ian van Bellen fitted my forward pattern. He was enormous, six feet tall and weighing 18 stone, and had plenty of experience even though during the previous season of 1980, when Bradford Northern (now Bradford Bulls) had won the First Division Championship, he had been used mainly as a substitute. I succeeded in luring him away from Odsal for £5,000 and the only problem I had was finding a shirt big enough to fit him. Of course, at that time, I had no conception of his future popularity with the Fulham supporters.

At the same time, I made an offer to Workington for Harry Beverley but, at that time, they wanted too much cash for him.

That was the story for the next few weeks. Too often clubs asked too much for players and, finally, Reg Bowden attacked them in the press. While I considered what he said to be true, I was concerned that Reggie's outburst would not help me with the clubs with whom I was already negotiating. However, at the time, I had been trying to sign Harold Box and Keith Bell from Second Division champions

18

Featherstone Rovers, only to find the asking prices were £25,000 and £30,000 respectively. The honeymoon was over. I could expect no favours, some clubs were no longer trying to help us, they considered we had money and were going to try and bleed us for every penny we had. I was determined that they would not succeed.

My next signing was one of my most difficult. David Hull was on offer at Widnes for £22,000, which I considered too expensive. Eventually, the fee for the loose-forward was cut to £16,000. I still considered this excessive but after letting Reg Bowden join us, they were not prepared to grant any favours. "£16,000 or nowt," was their reaction. In the end, I settled for the fee Widnes wanted and it proved that the going was likely to get tougher still.

My next approach was for Ian Thompson, the Workington Town centre, who was offered to me at £22,000. They were not prepared to compromise, neither was I prepared to pay that amount. Ridiculous figures of this nature were becoming commonplace and when you take into consideration that I bought Noonan for £4,000, they were impractical. Instead, on Reg's recommendation, I returned to Widnes for David Allen, a utility player, who had made a handful of appearances for the Cheshire side's first team and had suffered badly through injuries. I had never seen him play but Reg had a high opinion of the lad and so I laid out £2,000. Money well spent! Later, in training, it was obvious he was a bargain and during the season he was to prove priceless.

My last member of the gang of 10 was my first Rugby Union signing, Adrian Cambriani, just 18 years old, from Swansea, where he played for the Penlan club. Cambriani was in the same mould as Welsh Rugby League and former Union star winger John Bevan, a powerful, determined player, superb balance, fast and strong with enormous potential.

I had been watching him for 18 months with a view to signing him for Warrington, and I was concerned as to whether he would turn professional and also whether I might be beaten to the post by another club. The lad had played international Rugby Union for the Wales youth side against England at Bridgend and, to my mind, had been the outstanding player. I understand he had been equally impressive on the 1980 Welsh youth side tour to South Africa. I was faced with the fact that another team, if they saw him and were able to, might persuade him to sign for them, he was so good. I waited patiently for his return from Johannesburg and contacted him at the first opportunity .

At first he was a little dubious. Not surprisingly, he was worried that he would be cast on the rubbish heap at 18 if he failed to make the grade at Rugby League because one thing was certain, Rugby Union would not have him back, but I knew this boy could only succeed. In those days, Union was still an amateur sport - once a player turned professional at Rugby League, they were banned by the Rugby Union authorities from playing their game.

I invited him to come and stay with me for a couple of weekends and train with the players. Eventually, he agreed to sign. At 18, he was one of the young players I needed in the side to give me the balance I required.

I promised him he would play Rugby League for his country within a maximum of two years. He played for Wales against France on 31 January 1981 - six months after signing. Turning professional was a big step for the lad but he turned out to be everything I thought he was. He went on to play for Fulham for seven years and was one of the club's top try scorers.

Adrian was not the only Rugby Union player I considered in those early days but, in my eyes, he was the best. Other players included Phil Ford, the Cardiff winger, who eventually switched to League at Warrington and Clive Woodward of Leicester and England, who went on to coach England, and many others, whose confidences I would not wish to betray. Peter Morgan, the Llanelli back who has played for Wales on several occasions was another player I talked to but, after the briefest of discussions, I decided his attitude was not right for Fulham.

It was not a one way process. Several Rugby Union players offered themselves to me. One was Paul Ringer, the Welsh flanker, who made an approach to me through a representative.

On three occasions, Ringer, I was told, was ready to change codes as a result of the hard time he had been given by the press and television. It was at that time, you may remember, that he had been banned from playing for his country after being sent off against England at Twickenham.

Never being one to close any door firmly shut until I have been fully convinced that the deal would not suit Fulham, I took his telephone number and attempted to call Ringer three times. Each time he was out and so I dropped the idea.

Ringer was never likely to be an asset to Fulham. At thirty-four, I considered he was too old to change to Rugby League. At the most we could get two years service for a large fee and a minimum of one of those years would have been spent learning the game. I was looking for promising Rugby Union players aged 20 or 21, not older than 30. However, Paul Ringer did switch to Rugby League the next year with new club Cardiff Blue Dragons.

So, on 22 July, our "gang of 10" signed players assembled for their first training session at the Golborne Sports Club in Leigh, just off the East Lancashire Road. There was an air of excitement and an air of determination to do well. It was a strange feeling, similar to voyagers preparing for an expedition. With seven weeks to the start of the season, I needed seven more players but, for the time being, all attention was on the first 10 who had just been joined by several amateurs, including a young player called Tony Kinsey.

Roy Lester

John Risman

Fulham captain Tony Karalius (on left) before playing Dewsbury
at Craven Cottage

Adrian Cambriani

Tony Gourley

Chapter 4: Bookies and more players

The side was taking shape and nobody knew that better than the bookmakers. Before I had even signed a player I went to a local bookie in Leigh and asked for the odds on Fulham gaining promotion. He looked at me and laughed: "When you start signing some players, come back and I will see what I can do for you."

Return I did, after the early players had joined us. Again the bookie laughed: "Evens for the title, odds on for promotion." I kept my money. The bookie, after obviously doing his homework, had recognised the potential at Craven Cottage.

But, even so, we could still only field a side of 10 players. It was the start of August, seven weeks to the opening day and more than £80,000 of the original £100,000 had already been spent. It was time to return to Ernie Clay and ask for more cash. I explained that we could pick up free-transfer men and older players for the remaining £20,000 but that would not guarantee promotion. I needed long-term class signings.

Once again, credit to the man, he gave the go-ahead to use more cash. If that money had not been available, I could always accept the offers I had received to borrow players from clubs such as Second Division Blackpool, and First Division Warrington and St. Helens who were all keen to make sure Fulham was successful.

However, the cash was there and he had been expecting me to return for more. When we first met at his home in Surrey, I had told him that I thought I would need £425,000 in the first three years to be a force in the game, so the plea for extra funds came as no real surprise to him.

Ironically, I only needed £1,000 for my next signing. Reg Bowden had brought a 19-year-old boy, Tony Kinsey, who was the Widnes colts captain, to Golborne. I watched him train on two occasions only and agreed with Reg that at £1,000, Kinsey was a gamble worth taking. In our first season he played in six positions for Fulham, including scrum-half, after Reg was injured against Leeds in the John Player Trophy. That day, he ran Kevin Dick, an international halfback, ragged.

Our next venture into the transfer market was not so successful. Graham Walters, a Welsh international, playing for First Division giants Hull, was unsettled on Humberside and for a fee of £14,000 had agreed to join us. Unfortunately, for us, he settled his differences at Hull, moved into a new house and after a long deliberation, decided to stay put. Whenever I saw Walters he impressed me and, to the player's credit, he wrote me a long letter explaining his reasons for staying at The Boulevard. However, it may well have been a blessing in disguise, because he had a nondescript season in 1980-81 and made few appearances for Hull.

Whilst this wrangle was going on, Widnes had problems of their own. Mal Aspey, their international centre, and David Eckersley, the Great Britain test player, had both asked for a transfer. Widnes refused Aspey a move and he immediately quit the club, while the Naughton Park committee upset Eckersley by placing a £25,000 price tag on him.

But it was to Wigan, not Widnes, I moved next, for John Wood the Great Britain under-24 international. He had been out for two years with a badly fractured elbow. The deal, it seemed, had gone through smoothly. I agreed terms with their chairman Harry Gostelow at £7,500 for the player, but the night before I was due to sign Wood, Wigan had a special board meeting at which Gostelow was replaced as chairman by Jack Hilton and the whole deal had to be renegotiated.

Hilton did not want to let Wood leave Wigan. The player, however, considered that he had been poorly treated by the Lancashire club and was equally determined that he would not play for them again. In those circumstances, Hilton decided to cut his losses and allow us to sign Wood who, I considered, was a certainty for Great Britain in the future. This time, there was a small change in the fee Wigan wanted.

Jack Hilton now wanted £25,000 but after a great deal of negotiation, £18,000 was accepted and agreed. Even though the original asking price had increased enormously, I realised I could not have bought a player as good as Wood, for that price, anywhere else. I was content and satisfied with my business transaction. Wood was joined in our pack by Tony Gourley from Salford who cost £13,000.

At the time, I knew they were short of cash, despite just having finished fourth in the First Division and Ray Hatton, Oldham's coach, was also interested in Gourley. However, Ray would not pay the fee of £13,000 that Salford were demanding. I decided that I would have to have Gourley, a real grafter, and one of the best tacklers in Rugby League. I paid Salford their price and Tony Gourley joined Fulham.

While these two deals were being clinched, Widnes were still arguing with Aspey and Eckersley. In the end, we stepped in and much to the Widnes fans' disapproval, signed the pair for £27,000. I am convinced that David Eckersley would not have joined us if Reg Bowden had not been with Fulham, but Mal Aspey may well have still moved to Craven Cottage.

People have talked about us being a Widnes B team and stealing players from Naughton Park but nothing could have been further from the truth. When I first planned the Fulham venture, I drew up a side I would like to sign. Of the Widnes players we had now, only Bowden and Hull were on that list. Bowden was always the first choice as player/coach and Hull had struggled to keep a first team place at Widnes and was on the transfer list.

David Eckersley, under pressure from David Moran and Mick Burke, was no longer a first team regular and his desire for first team football led him to ask for a move. Mal Aspey, although still a regular, was another player whose place was threatened by the galaxy of younger, potential stars at Widnes. Mal also asked for a transfer and was eager to jump at the chance of becoming assistant-coach at Craven Cottage.

As stated previously, David Allen had only played a small number of games for the first team in the eight years he had been with "The Chemics". In particular, the previous season, most of the time, he had spent on the treatment bench or in the A team.

The sixth player was an amateur, Tony Kinsey, who was considered by the Widnes club to be not good enough to become a professional. He was not signed on by them, despite being the captain of the Widnes colts side.

The season was now drawing closer and we were still two players short of the 17 I needed to face Wigan safely in the opening match of the season at Craven Cottage on 14 September.

I brought the expenditure to £140,000 by crossing the Pennines, to Featherstone Rovers, for their classy back, Neil Tuffs. He was another player who had suffered through injury and was now available, with the experience of 250 first team matches, for a fee of £6,000. I now had 16 players but Tony Kinsey was getting married on Saturday 13 September, the day before our season started and I knew I needed one more player to provide cover in the event of a last-minute hitch. It was not until the last moment that I finally acquired my man. I returned to Workington and agreed to pay £18,000 for Harry Beverley on Friday 12 September, just 48 hours before the big match with Wigan at Craven Cottage.

Harry was a vital signing - completed in front of a *Daily Mail* photographer in the dining room of my home at Glazebury. We now had back-up for every position and every eventuality. I never intended Harry to play against Wigan but he was always ready to step in should something go wrong.

I had tried to sign him for Warrington when he moved from Dewsbury to Cumbria, but had failed on that occasion. This time, although the original Workington asking price had been in the region of £25,000, we managed a compromise. At last I could sleep easy. Harry Beverley had been that all-important sedative. The whole of the sporting world was to be focused on Craven Cottage on 14 September, and Harry was the man, although not playing, who would make sure nothing went wrong.

The "wheeling and dealing" was completed and, looking back, I don't think I would have done anything different in similar circumstances. Maybe one or two names would be different if I had had more cash and more time, but, all-in-all, I was convinced that it was a job well done, not only for Fulham, but also for the sport of Rugby League.

If I had gone mad, flashing money all around the country, buying up big names, at inflated prices, we would have damaged the game we were trying so desperately to promote and expand.

I can honestly say that, although in several deals we did not see eye-to-eye on prices, I feel that Fulham did not upset anyone, except possibly the other Second Division promotion contenders, in our transfer activities. Various people had told us that there could be no progress without casualties, but these did not materialise. Struggling clubs Doncaster and Huyton were always thought to be the likely cannon fodder for the new Fulham Rugby League Club, however, I considered I had bought well and sensibly and the regulars at Tattersfield, Doncaster and Alt Park, Huyton, I assume, let out a sigh of relief. It was a double bonus for Rugby League, David Oxley and Jack Myerscough, I considered, would be grateful. Lunacy in the transfer market would have taken down more clubs financially than Huyton and Doncaster.

I am convinced that I could do it all again. The prices, more than likely, would be higher and maybe it would be a little tougher to get the right players but, in the end, I believe the result, taking into account the help I had received from many clubs such as Warrington, Widnes, St Helens and Salford, could be repeated. However, at Fulham, I still had to find out whether the commitment, enthusiasm and hard work was to be rewarded. The proof of the pudding could not have been much harder.

Over 80 minutes against Wigan, one of Rugby League's great names, the destiny of Rugby League in the south was to be decided. The moment of truth had arrived.

Another historic step:

The Rugby Football League Council
Minutes of meeting 6ᵗʰ August 1980

"It was proposed by Blackpool Borough, seconded by Barrow, and unanimously agreed to admit Fulham R.L.F.C. to Associate Membership of the Council."

Press day:
Top: Tony Gourley and Ian van Bellen with Malcolm Macdonald
Bottom: The front row: Roy Lester, Tony Karalius and Ian van Bellen with a couple of models in the second row

28

Chapter 5: The big day

Just 10 days before the start of the season nobody was left under any illusions about how much interest the Fulham venture had already attracted. It was 4 September, the press open day at Craven Cottage and it seemed as though everybody was there. Cameras, microphones and notebooks were everywhere. Everyone from the sports editors and columnists of the national papers to the most junior reporters from the locals were there. It was a little before 11a.m. when the players trotted through the autumn mist that was rolling off the banks of the Thames and into the glare of the publicity machine.

It was bewildering for most of them and it was also their first standing ovation, because, as the team ran out in their new, impressive all black strip with a white chevron, their wives and girlfriends, who were waiting in the main stand, spontaneously rose to their feet and began clapping and cheering. The press felt obliged to follow suit. Then the barrage of questions began. "Would the plan succeed? What about Wigan? Who is Reg Bowden? Which one is Adrian Cambriani?"

I was amazed at the number of people who turned up. I realised that if you laid on free drinks and food, sooner or later, one or two press boys would arrive but I, along with the caterers and administrative staff, were caught off-guard by the interest. An indication of the size of the gathering came when the buffet ran out, with many people still unserved, and new sets of press details had to be photocopied after the original ones were snapped up.

The players were elated at the response and coped with the occasion superbly and one or two even had time to enjoy themselves. No one more than Ian van Bellen, who had the privilege of pulling off the first tackle for Fulham - two attractive models who had been organised by Malcolm MacDonald. As van Bellen posed for pictures, Alan Thompson of the *Daily Express* said to me, "My lad plays rugby but, compared to him, these men are giants. Why have you picked so many big forwards?"

"I have played behind a small pack and I know how difficult it is.

Big forwards win matches, we have big jerseys, so we may as well fill them," I replied.

After the press conference, the players streamed out of the ground realising the size of the task ahead of them, as did our groundstaff.

The poor groundstaff. For hours before the press arrived, they had grappled with the posts. They used scaffolding up to erect them and, without exaggeration, the whole operation took almost three hours. Later, after months of practice, it took a mere 30 minutes with a swivel joint, an invention we designed. But the posts were not the only problem. New turf had to be laid behind the goals so that the football post sockets and the rugby post sockets were on the same line. Football players would not have been amused if, with the goal at their mercy, they suddenly slipped into the hole made by the rugby posts, nor would any visiting manager if one of his million pound players broke his ankle and so the problem had to be overcome.

After several conferences to consider Astroturf, it was decided that natural turf would be better for the in-goal area and so, with only a few weeks left before the season started, the new surface was laid. The groundsmen also had to experiment with dye to cover up the rugby or football line markings. After several enquiries, an old friend was chosen. We used a green vegetable dye that would not damage the turf. The same dye is also at Wembley Stadium.

As well as recruiting a team, we needed backroom staff and luckily, I managed to bring in Gordon Pinkney, a friend of Reg Bowden, who was with Huyton RLFC, to share the kitman duties with Jack Casey, who was our administrator based in the north and had a background in professional football. I also employed Alf Minshull as our timekeeper and as cook on the team coach. With the backroom staff ready, the pitch ready and the team ready, now that Beverley had been signed, I crossed my fingers and hoped that fortune would favour the bold.

The week up to the start of the season was hectic. Reg and I travelled to watch Wigan play Widnes in the semi-final of the Lancashire Cup. Widnes were the previous season's runners-up in the First Division,. Wigan won and many people, including Brian Batty of the *Daily Mail*, came up to us and said: "you've got a hell of a job on your hands now, haven't you?" We said nothing but we thought we had been watching two poor sides and knew we had a great chance of victory against Wigan. We were confident.

It was the second time that we had watched Wigan. The first time was in the previous round of the Lancashire Cup when they played Rochdale. I took Adrian Cambriani along with me, to show him Jim Hornby, the Wigan and Great Britain under-24 winger, a player he was likely to face in the opening game. It was also a chance for him to become familiar with the rules. Cambriani was not greatly impressed by Hornby. "He'll get little change out of me," was his attitude. However, Wigan's victory over Widnes must have given them a great lift. We were being referred to, in some areas, as Widnes B. If they were able to beat Widnes's first team, then they must have been certain they would thrash us. We knew differently. We were not Widnes B, we were a better side than the Widnes outfit that played in the semi-final and we were determined that Wigan would go home empty-handed.

Cambriani, of course, was the most inexperienced player on the books but, after watching him training, Reg and I were confident he would at least hold his own against Wigan. In fact, the whole side were so determined in training that I was certain Wigan would not live with them. But, even so, going in "cold" against one of the best teams in the League, would be a big test.

We had a deliberate policy not to play friendly matches in the run up to the season, even though I had offers from sides such as Hunslet and Salford. Reg wanted to play an amateur side, just for some match practice. Again, the idea was thrown out. "We do not need to play an amateur side to realise that an amateur player cannot stop Ian van Bellen 10 yards from the line," I told him. There were other considerations as well. With a small squad, I could not afford for someone to be injured in a meaningless encounter and, secondly, whether we played Salford or an amateur team, the gloss would be taken off the match with Wigan.

I told Reg that I knew it was a tall order, but he had to prepare the

31

side to play Wigan, and beat them, without a warm-up. And I didn't want anybody watching us beforehand. "Anyone who wants to watch Fulham will have to come on 14 September and pay to go through the turnstiles," I demanded. With credit to Reg, he reacted in the way I thought. "If that is how it has to be, then that is good enough for me," he said.

As the team prepared, it was obvious they were going to be in great shape and I forecast that we would be promoted. Many doubted me, but I was certain. The only unknown factor, as far as I was concerned, was the crowd. My biggest worry was that more people would have attended the press conference than the first match. The crowd was always the worry. Would anyone come? I am sure some people would come to the Wigan game just to be part of history. It was the other matches that would be the unknown quantity, especially if the unthinkable happened and we lost the opener. The thought of losing never really crossed the minds of the players. They had a determination to win and to overcome everything in their path.

The pressure never seemed to get to the players, even though the eyes of the whole sporting nation was on Craven Cottage. People were waiting for the chance to say "I told you so" if we lost, whilst others were waiting eagerly to acclaim an overnight sensation. No matter what happened, someone was going to rejoice, but the players, if affected by the attention, managed to hide it well. The uncanny part about the build-up to the game was the silence amongst the team.

Normally, they were a joking, noisy bunch but when they boarded the coach at the Greyhound Hotel, on the East Lancashire Road, Leigh on Saturday 13 September, we could not get a peep out of them. Their minds were firmly focused on one thing - beating Wigan - and nothing anyone said or did around them was likely to interfere with that determination.

It seemed like a lifetime before we reached Milton Keynes where we stayed for the first and, as it happened, the last time. It was a college with very basic accommodation and minimal home comforts. Some of the players complained that it was like a prisoner-of-war camp, so, after that, we stayed at the Ladbroke Mercury Hotel in

Watford, which proved far more pleasant. As I left on the Saturday afternoon for London, where I was to spend the evening with guests from all walks of the sporting public, the players were running out for their training session. As I drove away, I thought, "There's no way that Wigan can beat us tomorrow. No way in the world."

Spending the night away from the squad was more worrying than being with them. The time passed slowly and I kept thinking, "I wonder if someone has been injured?" Fortunately, the telephone never rang. We had reached the day of reckoning unscathed.

I think that the Sunday morning must rate as one of the longest and most agonising waits in my life. It was similar to a father waiting for his first child to be born. Would everything work out all right? As it happens, we had a birth in the family on the big day. At my Glazebury home, earlier in the summer, we found some duck eggs that had been abandoned. We decided that we should hatch them in an incubator. Surprise, surprise, on the day of the Wigan game, the ducklings were born and my wife called them Roy, Reggie and Korky after three of the first players I signed - Lester, Bowden and MacCorquodale.

Meanwhile, I drove the short distance from my hotel in Kensington to Craven Cottage, arriving about 10am - five hours to the kick-off. It really seemed like five years. I opened the good luck messages, including one from Tommy Docherty, the controversial Preston North End and former Manchester United, Chelsea and Queens Park Rangers football manager. As usual, when you are looking for something to pass the time, it only took minutes. Checking arrangements, kit, tickets and catering is a thankless task. The more you check, the more you are convinced something is going wrong. While I was carrying out these tasks, I could not help thinking, "Has someone woken up feeling ill?" "Has someone fallen down the stairs?" The worry would not be over until they actually arrived at the ground. All the little problems were ironed out. All the tickets were arranged - the last thing the team wanted was to be rushing around sorting out tickets for family and friends.

All the time I kept looking down Stevenage Road, which runs alongside Craven Cottage, hoping and praying that someone would actually come to watch. Gradually coaches began to arrive and slowly people started to drift into the ground.

Despite the huge crowd, the gate receipts appeared low. But it must be remembered that, as with the match against Bradford Northern, the attendance included those with complimentary tickets. We invited for free the whole of the Rugby Football League, including the directors, council members and staff, along with Chelsea pensioners, Fulham football season ticket holders and several hundred school children. They enjoyed the afternoon and many returned to future matches.

Then, at last, the players arrived, all fit and well and looking very intense. Most were hardened professionals - they would not let the occasion spoil their game, they would more likely rise to it. They knew what I required of them and they were determined not to let anyone down, least of all themselves.

As I repeatedly left the dressing room to watch the fans streaming in, there were last minute worries. "Would the referee have a bad day?" "Could a couple of poor decisions ruin over a year's hard work?" As it turned out, I should not have had any worries. The referee, Fred Lindop, had a marvellous afternoon. I returned to the dressing room in time to give last words of encouragement to Reg and skipper, Tony Karalius. The whole team then stood up and began shaking each other by the hand. The team spirit for a side created in just ten weeks was incredible and a tribute to the players involved, especially Reg Bowden, who had demonstrated the player/coach attributes I had hoped he would. When they ran out into the September haze to the cheers of the 9,000 plus crowd, I actually felt sorry for Wigan. Imagine that, feeling sorry for the opponents. There was no way they could win.

Chapter 6: Wigan

Meanwhile, on the other side of the ground, in front of a packed Stevenage Road stand - the presentations were being made. First out were the former great Wigan players, Billy Boston, Joe Egan and Ernie Ashcroft. Then I remember a tremendous cheer as I led the players onto the field, where we were introduced to guest of honour Lord Peart, the Leader of the Opposition in the House of Lords and the Rugby League dignitaries.

Then, at last, with the roar of the 9,554 people welling up inside the ground, the moment I had waited two years for - Rugby League kicking off in London - took place. From that moment on, Wigan were dead. In the first five minutes, when Tony Gourley brought off two crunching, bone-shaking tackles, I knew there was no way we could lose.

Wigan - a mere shadow of the side that had beaten Widnes the Wednesday before - seemed to recognise this as we outran and outplayed them for long periods in the game. Points had to come. We won the first three scrums and Iain MacCorquodale was narrowly off target with the first penalty but in the 20th minute, when David Allen was fouled off the ball, MacCorquodale made no mistake. Striking the ball beautifully, it sailed between the posts. The romp had started and history was being made.

We continued to press forward in waves and in the 34th minute we crossed for our first try. The ball moved from Bowden, first to Gourley, then Aspey and finally Cambriani came haring down the touchline to go over in the corner.

MacCorquodale added the goal and Wigan were already on the ropes. The killer punch came on the stroke of half-time. MacCorquodale, playing probably his best game in Fulham colours, chipped the ball into the corner and Cambriani - who admitted later that he had not even been sure of the rules before the match - raced past the cover to score his second try. It was 10-0 at half-time.

The scrums were to our advantage, 9-2 in the first half and Tony Karalius, although 33 years of age, lapped up the exciting big match

Fond memories of 1980

I suppose it is fair to say that I never believed it would happen...
professional Rugby League on the banks of the River Thames just
a healthy punt kick from fashionable Chelsea! But back in 1980 it
actually happened and I was there for that first match against
Wigan at Craven Cottage.

That was back in the days when I was writing the Rugby League
column for the Sunday Mirror. I had worked all through the night
in Manchester helping compile the northern editions of the tabloid
newspaper and then dashed to catch and early morning train to
London for the match.

All thoughts of sleep were totally banished when I walked down
to Craven Cottage. I had never been to the West London Stadium
during my sports journalism carer and to me the place was all
about the first ever £100 per week soccer player Johnny Haynes.

But, by the end of that memorable first day, all I could think of
was the giant prop Ian van Bellen, a blond-haired Welsh winger
Adrian Cambriani and the incredible atmosphere of that win over
Wigan.

It seemed inconceivable that a proud northern club like Wigan
could lose out to a scratch team built over weeks by the club's
driving force Harold Genders.

While Wigan were not the force they are today the Central Park
men were still being seen as red hot favourites to win. But Reg
Bowden's boys got up to win and it is still one of my all-time
favourite Rugby League memories even though I spent more than
an hour after the game trying to find a tube station to take me back
to Euston Station.

John Huxley
Rugby Football League Media Manager
June 2000

Fulham versus Wigan - the programme from the first match

atmosphere and won them 7-4 in the second half. Substitute, Neil Tuffs, not to be outdone by Cambriani, also ran in two tries in the second half and, in the 70th minute, David Allen ran in the fifth, despite having Wigan full-back George Fairbairn - later to move to Hull Kingston Rovers for a record £72,000 transfer fee - hanging round his waist. MacCorquodale kicked two more goals and the Fulham score was rounded off with a by David Eckersley drop goal.

Wigan's only consolation was a try by Bernard Coyle, five minutes from time. It was converted by George Fairbairn, the Wigan player/coach, who said afterwards: "No excuses - they outplayed us in every department and they played all the football. I really hope that Fulham gain promotion... along with ourselves."

Jack Hilton, the Wigan chairman, was also gracious in defeat. In the boardroom, he came to congratulate me and said: "You did not beat us, you humiliated us."

Everything had gone like a dream. The 24-5 victory tasted sweet that evening. People had said we were too old, we had too many weak links. In the end, they were all proved wrong. Jack McNamara of the *Manchester Evening News* was one of the first to congratulate me afterwards. "I now realise, after watching that performance, why you bought every one of the players," he said. He had recognised that the balance was right. The experience of players such as Karalius, Bowden and Aspey matched with the enthusiastic running of men like Allen, Wood and Cambriani.

The celebrations went on long into the night and I am sure that a few of our players, together with the supporters who had carried us round on the marvellous emotional lap of honour, felt a little the worse for wear the next day. In fact, the only sore point of the whole weekend, which annoyed me considerably, was that Bob Wilson, the former Arsenal goalkeeper and self-styled sports expert, was of the opinion that Rugby League would never take off in London. I detected a note of concern, maybe his hallowed game of football felt threatened. In any event, what did he know about Rugby League, or for that matter, the Fulham venture? Yet he was prepared to dismiss it in one remark. I have always maintained that football can live together with

Press headlines from the big match:

Fulham start with glory and a fanfare

BOUNCING BABES!

fairy-tale start for Fulham

Fulham versus Wigan - the match ball signed by the Fulham players
(Photo: Peter Lush, courtesy Ron Snares)

Lord Peart meets the Fulham players before the Wigan match

Fulham versus Wigan: Reg Bowden about to pass

40

Top: Iain MacCorquodale kicks the first points
Bottom: Fulham 24 Wigan 5 - the final score

41

Rugby League and that London is large enough for both of us. His statement, to me at least, appeared to have a touch of small-mindedness.

Whatever Bob Wilson thought, however, there were other football personalities who felt the whole venture was a huge success, including Tommy Docherty. He told reporters afterwards: "I will enjoy it more when I know the rules but, on that evidence, it must be good if more soccer clubs follow Fulham's lead. I thoroughly enjoyed it - great entertainment!"

An Orient football supporter added, "It was marvellous. There was no hugging or kissing when they score or arguing with the referee. We are coming again."

The papers on the Monday morning summed the afternoon up. "Sunday best - Rugby League scores with capital show," exclaimed the *Daily Express*. "Clay has 9,554 reasons to hope," was the headline on Ian Woolridge's report on the Fulham phenomenon in the *Daily Mail*, while the *Daily Mirror* screamed: "Baby Bashers" (as we were the 'babies' of the league). Everyone was convinced. The gamble had worked. Most people who attended the match said, Fulham will not only be promoted, they would win the league. Winning the league was never our target, but promotion was. After the way we dealt with Wigan - "red hot" favourites for the Second Division crown - some people said they doubted if we would lose a Second Division match.

The result that afternoon was the most sought after in British sport for a long time. Rugby League, Association Football, Rugby Union, people who had no interest in Rugby League, wanted to know the score. It was a situation probably unequalled in the sport - even in the Challenge Cup Final.

However, possibly the players became a little blasé during the next week and were perhaps believed that they were unbeatable. If they were, they soon received a nasty jolt to their egos.

Keighley have a nice ground, but in those days the Rugby League team had not always been the most successful. On 21 September 1980, they were looking forward to an historic event - the visit of the new boys, Fulham. These were the Londoners, who were proud from their victory against Wigan. They were the team the press had said would not lose a match. How wrong they were. We were slaughtered 24-13. We had convinced ourselves that all we had to do was turn up. Nobody could beat us, so we thought. Nobody except Keighley, as we discovered.

The match was like a cup tie. We had reversed roles in a week. No longer were we the side with something to prove. We were the side that everyone wanted to beat. Keighley gave us a taste of things to come throughout the rest of the winter. If we were under any illusion that the Second Division was going to be a cake walk, it ended right there, at Lawkholme Lane. It was something we had never imagined. The one blind spot in all our planning. We had not realised how much supposedly poor sides could raise their game.

Keighley must have enjoyed playing the new additions to the Rugby League, for the following season, they thrashed Cardiff City in the second match of the season - after Cardiff had narrowly lost their first match against another of Rugby League's great traditional clubs - Salford.

In a week, Fulham had turned from heroes to no-hopers but we were convinced that we could still take the league by storm. The defeat was the best thing that could have happened to us. We were going into matches now with our eyes wide open.

We also started to strengthen the playing squad. I signed Chris Ganley from Warrington. He had played there for three years when I was a director and played full-back or centre. In November, we made another recruit from Rugby Union, forward Peter Souto, who had been in the Welsh international squad in 1979 joined us from Cardiff RUFC. Chris was 22 and Peter 20 so they were both younger additions to the squad.

New players: Full-back Chris Ganley (top) and forwards Peter Souto (middle) and Martin Herdman (bottom)

Chapter 7: Cup magic

With every cup competition, there is a special magic, a special attraction and the John Player Trophy was certainly no different. If anything, for Fulham, it was especially exciting - it was the club's first venture into cup football. We had missed the chance to enter the Lancashire Cup as it is organised at the end of the previous season. Also, we did not have a team signed by then. In future years we played in the Lancashire Cup as our roots were in that area. As there were more teams in Yorkshire than Lancashire it suited the Rugby League for us to enter the Lancashire Cup.

And what a start... First Division Rugby League giants Leeds, at home on 23 November. It was an ironic pairing, especially with all the help Jack Myerscough, the Leeds chairman and also, at that time, chairman of the Rugby League, had given us. He later told the story of the draw. He had been waiting with David Oxley in a Leeds television studio for the draw to begin when David commented beforehand, "It has to be Fulham for you". It was unbelievable, Jack drew out the Leeds ball and he immediately said to David: "Honestly, no fix."

My attitude was that any fixture at Craven Cottage would be good but, I think, perhaps, a gentler start than Leeds may have been preferred. In at the deep end was putting it mildly. As Colin Welland wrote in the match programme: "If Widnes are the Liverpool of Rugby League, Leeds must be the Manchester United. They have a special magical attraction." Their visit to Craven Cottage certainly proved that and the supporters' imagination was fired by the prospect.

It had been an impressive run-up. We had been unbeaten since the match at Keighley, including home victories over Swinton, Huddersfield and York, all by large margins, which meant morale was high. But there was still one dark cloud on the horizon and that was the suspension of Roy Lester, who had been sent off against York following an incident with Pat McDermott. The obvious result was that he felt the odd man out that day and moped around dejectedly, but the buoyancy of the remainder of the squad created a marvellous atmosphere in the dressing room. Once again, the players had recaptured the spirit and drive of the opening match against Wigan and I knew this was to be our day.

Carefully executed planning by, for the most part, experienced players and officials, who had seen Leeds on several occasions, did not alter the fact that, although they were having a poor time in the league, the man to charge them up for a cup tie was their coach, Syd Hynes. In the league, the omens certainly seemed to be swinging back to Leeds after their sparkling victory over Barrow. However, I was still convinced we could win. Although there were possible weaknesses in the backs caused both by injuries and advancing years, I felt we had an overall advantage with our larger and more powerful forwards.

Leeds, even for all their big match experience, did seem to be affected by the atmosphere at Craven Cottage. A total of 12,583 fans - a John Player First Round competition record - crammed into the stadium on a cold, dark November afternoon.

From the start, Fulham dictated the game with committed running, forward aggression and fierce tackling. Leeds, for long periods, were pinned down on the defensive but, finally, that defence was broken in the first half by David Eckersley - star of the afternoon - who produced two drop goals, together with Iain MacCorquodale, who scored two further penalties and who had, at that time, scored in every match of the season. But Leeds came bouncing back and camped on the Fulham line for what seemed like an eternity with every scrum cheered on by our supporters and every tackle cheered.

Leeds trooped off at half time, drained. All their efforts and energies had been in vain, the Fulham line was still intact. The second half still belonged to Fulham as Cambriani started a move in the 65th minute with a break for the Leeds line and he found Eckersley in support. He slipped the ball to David, who did the rest, jinking round tackle after tackle before forcing his way over the line. Shortly after, the Leeds defence looked in tatters as Neil Hague and Kevin Dick just prevented Derek Noonan adding another try. However, Leeds did manage a consolation try by Graham Eccles, eight minutes from time to make the score 9-3 but nothing was going to deny us our victory and moment of glory - the greatest achievement, so far, in the short history of the Fulham club, and this was endorsed by the reception the players received from the delighted crowd.

Rugby League, undoubtedly, is a great leveller. One minute you are up, the next you are down. One minute you are on top, the next on the bottom and, in hindsight at that Leeds match, there were two disappointments and one high spot.

The high spot was Tony Kinsey's performance, when he replaced the injured Reg Bowden at scrum-half after 52 minutes. Kinsey, you may remember, was told by Widnes that he would never make the grade, yet he gave Kevin Dick, an international scrum-half, a torrid time and if anyone had been asked, as a neutral observer, to choose the international back, they would surely have plumped for Tony. He set up dummies, made breaks and became the general of operations. He was outstanding. After 65 minutes, Dick retired with a recurrence of a thigh injury. It was a case of adding injury to insult. Dick said afterwards: "The atmosphere was tremendous, we have never experienced anything like that."

The two disappointments, however, were injuries to both Reg and Harry Beverley. They had to be substituted during the match and were suffering from identical rib cartilage injuries. Amid the scenes of jubilation in the dressing room afterwards, Reg revealed his feeling that he would miss the next round and Harry was not confident either. In any event, both would be unfit to play in the following week's league game at Wigan.

When the draw for the second round of the John Player Trophy was made the following day and we were paired with Leigh at Hilton Park, it appeared fate had taken a major hand. As Reg joked in the press: "We only train a mile from Leigh's ground and I hope the players remember that it is a real match, not a training session when we get there."

Meanwhile, Alex Murphy, who had previously coached Warrington, had taken over as manager of Leigh. There was no love lost between the two of us and he would be all out to win. I had been a director at Warrington when his contract as the club's coach was terminated. In the Leigh local paper he was quoted as saying, "I am looking forward to crossing swords with Harold Genders again," and that he certainly did.

However, first we had to travel with the depleted squad for a top-of-the-table match against Wigan at Central Park and it seemed that this was to set the tempo for the next few weeks. It was an ill-tempered game, with Wigan all out for revenge after their humiliation at the historic first match. With Bowden and Beverley both out, the last thing we really wanted, or needed, was an injury but, sure enough, after only five minutes, Derek Noonan was carried off with a broken jaw, sustained in an off-the-ball tackle.

Although Derek didn't play again for 11 weeks, we didn't even received a penalty for the offence, as the referee and touch judges took no action and, to add insult to injury, Cambriani had a try disallowed at a crucial time in the match.

In the second half, however, came the real disappointment. With 52 minutes gone, Ian van Bellen was tackled by Steve O'Neill, the Wigan prop and as Ian tried to clamber up to play the ball, O'Neill rolled over holding his face. The touch judge came onto the field and Billy Thompson, the referee, sent van Bellen off for what he described in his dismissal report as "viciously kicking out at O'Neill and catching him in the face". In support of a Rugby League directive that referees should satisfy themselves that injuries to players had actually occurred, I went to Mr. Thompson's dressing room after the match and asked him to inspect O'Neill's face for marks. He declined, but when Ian spoke to O'Neill, Steve agreed that he should not have been sent off and even promised to write a letter in his defence. The letter never arrived.

We left Central Park both disgruntled and dejected but well beaten. We had no qualms about the result, only the bad tempered nature of the game.

Derek Noonan had been taken to hospital and our worst fears were confirmed when a specialist said he would be out of the game for six weeks or longer. Looking at our injury list, it became more and more obvious that Reg would have to play against Leigh.

During the week running up to the Leigh game, we had a desperate scramble to get Reg fit. Later we were accused of trying to pull "a fast one", but we really did not know, until the final moment, whether he would play or not.

The squad were a little downhearted during the build-up to the match because there were so many injuries and, with the disciplinary matters hanging over us, it would be a real task to lift them for the second round tie.

If Leeds was the high point of the season, then Leigh was surely the lowest. The match was shrouded in controversy. Unfortunately, it was nothing to do with anything that happened on the field.

The players met at the Greyhound Motel, Leigh, as usual, on the Sunday morning of 7 December, and we drove to Leigh's Hilton Park ground - still not certain Reg would play. During the short coach journey, I chatted to Reg and we came to the same conclusion. We thought he would have to play but the final decision would be left as late as possible. As the coach drew into the ground, our problems began. First, there were not enough tickets for the wives, girlfriends, parents and friends of the players - a courtesy normally afforded to a visiting side.

With only 30 minutes to the kick-off, the players were faced with a desperate search for tickets. Adrian Cambriani's parents, who had travelled all the way from Swansea were finally left to stand behind the posts. It certainly was not the best preparation for an important cup tie and, finally, when the team found their way to the dressing room, the customary match programmes for the players totalled six. We were told by the Leigh officials that 24 had been put in the dressing room. The fact remained, however, that as far as the Fulham players were concerned, when they entered, that was not the case.

It was not only the players who were having their difficulties, because, in the directors' box, more tickets had been issued than there were seats available. Brian Dalton, the Fulham financial director, and his wife, entered the box to find it full. The only two seats remaining were reserved. Brian , however, insisted that as a Fulham director, he was entitled to a seat and he and his wife sat down. Kenneth Wolstenholme, the former television commentator and Fulham's guest, was forced to sit on a stool in the aisle.

On the field, things went even worse. Reg and Harry, both heavily strapped, agreed to play but were never in their best form. In fact, Reg made the error which finally gave Leigh the game, when his misdirected pass was intercepted by Les Wall and Billy Platt scored a try. John Woods's conversion decided the contest. Our consolation was a Ganley try and three MacCorquodale goals, so we lost 17-9.

However, if defeat were not enough, we also added Tony Karalius and Tony Gourley to the casualty list. Karalius's injury was the worse. He damaged a thigh muscle that was to keep him out of the game for more than a month. Karalius's injury also brought home our desperate need for a regular second-string hooker. Tony Kinsey had done a marvellous job as stand-by, but even he would be the first to admit, it was not really his position.

To add more fuel to the fire, there were two more unsavoury incidents after the match. Our players had been issued with only 22 bar tickets, which did not cover the players' wives as well as themselves. There were more unpleasant moments when Ian van Bellen and Mal Aspey virtually had to fight with the doorman to gain admission. It should be remembered that Mal Aspey had actually played and was our assistant player/coach. I was called to sort the situation out.

We finally managed to obtain 18 extra tickets, after a 20 minute wait in the cold but, Mrs Pinkney, the kit-man's wife, had to wait on the coach for 45 minutes until Reg obtained a ticket for her.

Then, in the board room, I became the target for a one-sided slanging match from Alex Murphy. I say one-sided, because I chose to ignore him completely. Instead, I appealed to Brian Bowman, the Leigh chairman, and in receiving no satisfaction, I put my glass of half-drunk whisky on the bar and left the room. Our John Player Trophy run, which had begun so well, had suddenly turned so sour.

A fortnight later, I wrote to Leigh complaining about Alex Murphy's attitude and received a remarkable letter in return from Brian Bowman. He wrote: "I thought your letter had been sent to the wrong address and I thought you meant to have sent it to *Billy's*

Weekly Liar" (a newspaper full of lies hat used to be printed during the high season in Blackpool). In his letter, Mr. Bowman said we received 44 tickets, six extra box tickets and Reg was given 21 stand tickets, approximately 50 ground tickets and 63 bar tickets. This did not match the tally we calculated. On the clash with Alex Murphy in the board room, he said that he thought it was something that went back to our days together at Warrington.

He was also angry that the press did not know the exact strength of our team before they ran out onto the field. "We may have had a bigger gate if you had," he said. The truth was that we did not know right until the last minute who was going to play and it was not a deliberate attempt to hoodwink anyone.

Because I had not received a satisfactory answer, I decided to write to the Rugby Football League but, before this was possible, news of the incident between myself and Alex Murphy had been leaked to the *Sunday People* newspaper and, in an article by John Robinson, Murphy claimed he had nothing to apologise for. I wrote to David Oxley complaining that the report in which Murphy was quoted brought the game into disrepute. I waited for a reply, but nothing happened and eventually the curtain fell on a distressing occasion.

Despite this incident, I believe that Alex Murphy was the greatest Rugby League player I ever saw and a few years later we resolved our differences. I invited Alex to be the guest speaker at one of the annual trips to the Challenge Cup Final for our clients and staff that I organised for AMEC.

The defeat at Leigh was a blessing in one way, because it gave us a week without a game for the injuries to heal. Fortunately, Reg and Harry both came through the match without problems but Karalius and Gourley were ruled out of an important home match with Hunslet, just before Christmas. Hunslet, at that time,

The brochure from the AMEC cup final trip

were riding high in the league and it was vitally important that we beat them and beat them well. With some clinical finishing, we romped home 19-5 and put an end to Hunslet's dreams of First Division football. From that moment on, they slid slowly down the table.

With such a small squad and the number of injuries we had, it was important that new blood was found as quickly and cheaply as possible, and we knew exactly who we wanted. Both targets could be described as being bought from the bargain basement and both looked certain to have a big future in the game.

Londoner Martin Herdman, aged 24, was one of the many, many people who wrote to me when the club began, asking for a trial. But something struck me about his letter that made it stand out from all the rest. "You will not be disappointed if you come and watch me and you will not fail to be impressed," he wrote. We advised him leave his Rugby Union club, Orleans, and join the London amateur club Peckham RLFC to get in some practice and we would come along and watch him. He played for Peckham in the John Player Sevens before our match at Leigh, but with so many problems at Hilton Park, I am ashamed to admit, I did not watch him. Fortunately, Reg Bowden was watching and after 10 minutes, Reg pulled him to one side and told him all the things he was doing wrong, promising to return and watch him again.

Sure enough, Reg went back to see him and Martin was a star. He ripped through the amateur opposition, scoring four tries and making three others. Reg reported back - he thought we were on to something. "I was shattered not to be signed right away," said Martin later. York suddenly started to take an interest in him and we quickly invited him for a first team trial against Batley.

Also playing that day was Carl Radbone, a stand-off, who had travelled up each week from Penlan with Adrian Cambriani, for training. After a while, Carl started playing for an amateur Rugby League team near Widnes. Unfortunately, within ten minutes of his first amateur match in October, he broke his collar bone. In that time though, he showed enough promise. He burst through three or four tackles to score under the posts and then set up another sparkling move. The injury set him back a couple of months and it was only at the start of December that he began to return to full fitness. Against Batley at Craven Cottage on 28 December, both made their debuts and acquitted themselves superbly in a 15-5 victory and were signed up soon afterwards. Their careers, however, took very different paths.

The 1980 Fulham Christmas card: R for Rugby League, F for Football

Reg Bowden receives the October Coach of the Month
award from Harold Genders

Fulham shirt with players signatures from the Craven Cottage period
(Photo: Peter Lush, courtesy Ron Snares)

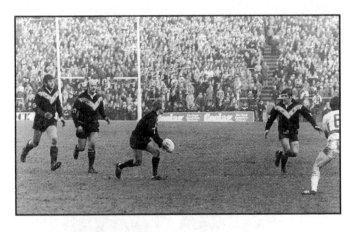

Fulham versus Wakefield Trinity in the Challenge Cup at Craven Cottage.
The crowd was the biggest for a London Rugby League
club match since the 1930s.

Chapter 8: Referees

Of course, referees are a necessary part of the game but, regrettably, sometimes they influence the result more than any player on the field. During my youth, I was taught that the best referee was one who was in total control without being obviously present. Unfortunately, some referees believe that spectators come to see them. I would like to emphasise, in my opinion, that the game is about players providing excitement and thrills and a good referee can contribute in a very large way by recognising that point.

Early in the season Fulham got the reputation - unfairly, I think - of being a dirty side. I have always considered rugby to be a man's game and it should always be played on a physical basis, but I have never encouraged dirty play and never will. However, much of our alleged bad reputation arose after the match against Swinton in September, our second match at Craven Cottage.

Swinton, easily beaten, claimed that we had achieved our victory through dirty play. In fact, to support their argument, I was told only two of their players had been fit to train the following Tuesday. Furthermore, they blamed us for the injury to Dave Nicholson that kept him out of Rugby League until we faced them again at their Station Road ground on a wet and muddy Sunday in February 1981.

It appeared that some referees believed Swinton's outrageous statements and I understand at a referees' meeting, considerable time was spent discussing Fulham. Whatever the truth of the situation, in my opinion, we appeared to have difficulties with referees and if there was a debatable decision, it always seemed to go against us.

Two of the prime examples were the matches against Wigan and Whitehaven. As I wrote earlier, at Central Park, the touch judge intervened and requested the referee to send Ian van Bellen off for kicking Steve O'Neill when even O'Neill admitted nothing had happened. However, earlier in the game, the referee and touch judges had completely ignored a late tackle on Derek Noonan which resulted in a broken jaw, which put him out of the game for 11 weeks.

Then, in January, we travelled to Whitehaven, never the easiest place to play and conditions were made worse by heavy overnight rain. As we slithered around in the mud, the referee refused to give us anything. Never in the game were we rewarded with a penalty in Whitehaven's half. That may not be unusual, but when you consider that Whitehaven had five kickable penalties awarded, it does seem a little unfair. Luckily, Ray Dutton only landed one but, even so, we went down 6-0.

Over the season, we conceded 258 penalties and were awarded only 165. Scrum penalties were 93-67 against us. This worked out at an average of 5.9 penalties for us to 9.2 against and in the scrum, 2.4 - 3.3 a match. When you add them together, the average match contained 8.3 penalties for Fulham and 12.5 for the opposition.

This meant that the opposition had more than four extra penalties a game and, if taken to the sixth tackle each time, it meant we were forced to make an extra 24 tackles - a high number. Despite this disadvantage, we often came through.

A typical match was against Doncaster at Tattersfield in October, when we were awarded four penalties to Doncaster's 18, however, we were still good enough to win 28-16.

Overall, the standard of refereeing was poor and if I had my way, I would pay Grade I referees the same match fee as the players and Grade II referees half that figure. Very few Rugby League followers would argue that a referee can make or break a game, particularly from an entertainment point of view and, therefore, a good referee can and does influence the number of spectators attending a match.

There is only one referee at each match and, therefore, the amount of extra money payable would be relatively small. Obviously, the extra money would not improve a bad referee but I do believe it would encourage greater numbers into the game with a higher standard of recruit into the game and this would benefit the sport considerably in the long term. I think there would be little argument that a good referee is obviously on a parallel with a good player and should, therefore, be paid accordingly .

Despite some people's view that refereeing is a 'vocation', I've always considered a man to be worthy of his hire. It is a professional game and we are living in a commercial world.

Two referees we had no complaints about were Fred Lindop, who gave such a splendid performance in our inaugural match against Wigan, which we won, and Ronnie Campbell, when we lost against Rochdale Hornets and Wakefield Trinity. For those three games, they were awarded the highest marks.

One of these games was probably our nightmare match of the season - at home to Rochdale on 11 January 1981. It was the only league match we lost at home all season and we had no-one to blame but ourselves. In the first five minutes we were 10-0 down and it is difficult to recover from that. Unfortunately, it was Carl Radbone, in his official debut, who was at fault for the first try. He was no more than a few feet from his own line when he threw a dreadful pass straight to Rochdale's John Gilmore, who scored.

Worse was to follow with further tries from Gilmore, Graham Gorvin and Henderson Gill. It seemed we would never learn. One of our biggest problems all season was trying to be overelaborate and over-entertaining. In doing so, we threw points away. The Rochdale game was the prime example. We won the scrums for the first time since playing Leigh in the John Player Cup but every time we got the ball, we gave it away.

It was unfortunate that we chose the day we won so much ball to be so generous. Iain MacCorquodale also had an off day. His 100% record of scoring in every match had fallen at Whitehaven and against Rochdale, he landed only one out of four easy attempts. It just was not our day and although we bounced back with two victories against Bramley and Huyton, which left us fourth in the table with games in hand, the most important win was probably at Hunslet on 1 February.

We were without Adrian Cambriani for only the second time in the season. Adrian had become the first player to be selected as an international while playing for Fulham, when he was chosen to play for Wales against France at Narbonne.

For Adrian, it was a dream come true. A moment he had been waiting for. When he first joined Fulham, he was determined to do well and prove himself because he was upset at the attitude of the

57

Welsh Rugby Union officials.

"I was determined to show them from the moment they dragged me out of the Welsh Rugby Union Centenary March. It was a march I had really been looking forward to as a member of the Welsh youth side that had toured South Africa so successfully. It was the biggest disappointment of my life," he said.

It should be explained that Adrian, on agreeing to sign for Fulham on the Wednesday prior to the Centenary March, had been refused permission by the Rugby Union hierarchy, to walk with the team that he had played with so ably up to that time.

Unfortunately, Adrian had no real chance to shine in the 23-5 thrashing by France but, even so, Reg Parker, the Welsh team manager and Blackpool director, said that he had been the ideal international. His chance to shine would come again, but it was a blow for us that he was missing from the line-up against Hunslet.

The game could not have been tighter. It was 11-11 with a minute to go and then David Eckersley dropped a goal that barely crept over the bar. It was now a six horse race for the four promotion places, between York, Wigan, Whitehaven, Huddersfield, Swinton and ourselves.

Swinton was to be our next trip and, unfortunately, after three successive wins, it was another defeat as we lost 9-13. On that day, however, we did manage to sign Joe Doherty from Rochdale Hornets for £4,000. Joe, a former Great Britain schools captain, was signed on a month's trial and then later on a full-time basis as cover at hooker for the ageing, and now injury prone, Tony Karalius. But, our search for a second, top-class hooker continued.

Chapter 9: French try

February 1981 will be a month etched in the memory of a Frenchman by the name of Jean-Marc Bourret. Bourret, 23, was comparatively unknown to the British sporting public until he was involved in a row between the French Rugby League and the Rugby Union authorities.

Bourret was the golden boy of French Rugby League and was even selected as the Adidas Golden Boot winner for 1980, which is the top international individual annual award. Then, just two days after scoring for the French Rugby League side against the New Zealand tourists, he defected to Rugby Union.

Rugby League officials in France were obviously dismayed that Bourret, who had played as a professional for Pia Rugby League side, should be allowed to appear in the amateur ranks with French club USAP Perpignan. Of course, this was before Union allowed professionalism in 1995 so in those days all their players were officially amateurs and thus banned from playing Rugby League. It was clear signing a leading professional Rugby League player was in breach of their own regulations, and was hypocritical.

After months of wrangling, David Oxley, the British Rugby League's secretary took up the case. "I do not want to persecute Bourret," he said, "but we must protect our interests in France."

Oxley brought the situation to the attention of the International Rugby Football Union and they agreed to debate the case at their meeting in Cardiff, the following month. It seemed cut and dried. Bourret, who was reported to have been paid up to £20,000 for turning 'amateur', would be banned from Rugby Union.

The French Rugby League had already indicated that they had no wish to welcome Bourret back into their ranks and that is where I thought Fulham could step in.

An exciting centre, Bourret was also a fine goalkicker and we knew that we would eventually have to find a replacement for Iain MacCorquodale. He had served us well and finished the season with 78 goals, but he was nearing the end of his career and he knew as well as we did that he was no longer up to First Division standard.

Bourret, the top French Rugby League player, would be the ideal replacement. The only problem was how to sign him and, if we did, whether he would be eligible to play in this country. I contacted the Rugby League and was given the 'all clear'. David Oxley said that he could see no problems if Bourret came to play in England and was enthusiastic about the idea of him joining Fulham.

Luckily, David Powell, my brother-in-law - who spoke excellent French - was flying to Paris the next day and so I asked him to try and arrange a meeting with Bourret.

Bourret, who worked in a bank in Perpignan, in the south of France, was in Paris on a banking course and so it seemed there would be no problems. Unfortunately, the course seemed more like a prison - no one was allowed out for the whole weekend. Finally, we got our message to him. His response was a mixture of apathy and surprise. He honestly believed that the French Rugby Union authorities would not suspend him and, therefore, he could see no reason for coming to London. His reply was typical of French Rugby Union. "How can I be a professional rugby player if I have always worked in a bank?"

French Rugby Union, it seems, has some unusual ideas about the definition of amateurism and professionalism. Bourret believed that if he did not earn his full-time living from Rugby League, then he could not be a professional.

No matter how many documents the French produced to show that he had played for cash, Bourret remained adamant that he was an amateur and said so forcibly under the headline, "Regrets, I have none," in the French sports paper, *L'Equipe*.

Still, we worked on him and in the end he said that if he was banned by the Rugby Union, he would consider our offer. London, he said, was the only place in England be would consider playing. We still had hope. Ernie Clay had taken to the idea and was desperately hoping that Bourret would sign and when he heard that Bourret finally had been suspended by the Union authorities telephoned me at 6am to pass on the news.

Unfortunately for Fulham, the suspension was only temporary to allow the French Rugby Union board to carry out an investigation into the matter. It was like the guilty judging the guilty and in the summer, Bourret, somehow, was cleared. As history has shown, though, we didn't give up on France. The next season, we returned there to sign Hussain M'Barki, a Moroccan Rugby Union star.

As one chase ended, another one began. I had been looking for a replacement for Tony Karalius for some time. Tony had promised me when he signed that he would give Fulham a season and it was clear that he was not going to be able to go beyond that pledge.

My thoughts turned to two players. One was John Dalgreen, at Warrington, who was recovering from surgery on a shoulder injury and the other was Alan McCurrie, at Wakefield.

Dalgreen, who eventually signed for us in May 1981, was still not match fit and so I turned my full attention to McCurrie. An instantly recognisable figure on the field, McCurrie looked older than his 29 years because of a shock of grey hair. This, I thought, was my man and I contacted Wakefield to see how much they wanted for him. At first, they did not want to know and then, finally, they set a fee around the £20,000 mark.

At that particular moment, that sort of cash was not available and the fact that we were unable to raise it was to have tremendous implications later in the month. As we hung fire on the deal, the draw was made for the first round of the Three Fives Challenge Cup. Who were we to play? Wakefield Trinity, the 1979 Challenge Cup runners up, with McCurrie in their team, at Craven Cottage.

Obviously, Wakefield were not then prepared to let McCurrie go. They did not want to sell him to us only for him to bring about their downfall in the Challenge Cup.

The failure to find the money at the right time cost us the tie and thousands of pounds in lost revenue for the later rounds. McCurrie had a wonderful match directing operations for Wakefield and they won 9-5 in front of a crowd of 15,013 on a glorious February afternoon. Again, as with our John Player Trophy defeat at Leigh, we helped our opponents.

From the start, the atmosphere did not seem quite right. In the dressing room, the players did not give the air of men who knew they were going to win. It was rather one of men who hoped they might win. No matter how much you talk to them, cajole them, shout at them, nothing can change it. As I strolled across the pitch to the dug-out, I realised that this was not going to be a repeat of the Leeds and Wigan triumphs.

I hoped that I would be wrong but, somehow, I could not see us winning. We managed to hold them early in the game and we were only trailing 4-0 at half time. Allan Agar - later to become Carlisle's coach - opened the scoring with a drop goal and then, after 17 minutes, Keith Smith, the former England Rugby Union international centre, sold our defence a perfect dummy to score a fine try.

Even at half time, we could have been in a better position, had MacCorquodale not missed two kickable penalties - one straight in front of the posts.

In the second half, we appeared to be getting on top when we blundered. As had so often happened in the past, a pass went astray. Agar intercepted from Mal Aspey and fed it to the stand-off, David Topliss, who raced like the wind into our half. Backing up was their substitute, Steve Diamond (who was to join the Craven Cottage side during the close season). Diamond cut across our half before feeding Andrew Fletcher, who raced over in the corner despite the despairing efforts of Chris Ganley, our talented full-back.

That was in the 67th minute and two minutes later, David Hull struck Agar and Diamond landed the penalty, making the score 9-0. Hull made amends with a try four minutes from time and although MacCorquodale landed the goal, Wakefield were out of sight.

The players were bitterly disappointed afterwards and realised that they only had themselves to blame. They gave away the ball too often - and against a good side, that is criminal.

The one good thing to come from the game was the return of Derek Noonan. He had been out since the Wigan match on 30 November and he tackled fiercely and bravely. His form that day was the bright spot.

We had had some worrying moments with Derek's jaw, none more so than at Christmas. He had been eating his lunch on Christmas Day with his jaw wired up, when it started to swell.

At first we thought that he had broken it again but a visit to the specialist early in the New Year revealed all, if not well, was satisfactory. It had been a long recovery and it was a little bit of a gamble to throw him in against Wakefield but, it had to be done. Luckily, it paid off. Derek came through without mishap and was able to finish the season.

Looking back on the year, I cannot help thinking that Derek's prime months were lost to us through the injury - an injury that had never even earned us a penalty. When he returned, after the Wakefield game he seemed to lack sharpness and towards the end of the year lost his place in the team. Wakefield and McCurrie went on to beat Halifax 18-8 in the next round before falling to Warrington in the quarter-finals.

For Fulham it was slightly different fare. We played Blackpool at home in the Second Division. The crowd was different as well. Instead of 15,000 plus - the third highest gate of the season in all Rugby League domestic competitions - we had to be content with 4,715, our lowest in the League.

I don't think Martin Herdman minded though. In front of Reg Parker, the Blackpool director and also Welsh team manager, he turned on a fine display. Parker was impressed and even more interested when he found out that Martin had a Welsh father.

To Martin's surprise, when the Welsh team was picked the following fortnight, he appeared in it. "I couldn't believe it," he said. Unexpected, certainly, but not undeserved.

Martin had put a lot of work into his game and had come a long way in a very short time. After four full matches and four as a substitute, he was in the Welsh squad.

The match must have been the most difficult one possible for him. Away to England at Hull Kingston Rovers' Craven Park on 18 March. Martin was named as a substitute and the story goes that he roomed with Colin Dixon. Not being shy, Martin impressed on Colin how much he wanted to play for Wales and so maybe it was a bit of a coincidence when Colin developed an injury after 62 minutes and Martin was called on.

He took his chance well and proved to many of the people in the stands that he had a marvellous future ahead of him. In fact, Paul Rylance of the *Daily Telegraph* said in his match report that Herdman, although in action for only 18 minutes, was probably one of Wales's outstanding players in a 17-4 defeat.

Two international players in our first season was impressive but the real business of promotion - our foremost ambition - had to be achieved. The next few matches were make or break. After the defeat at Swinton in February, we had continued winning in the league and by the middle of March were third, two points behind Wigan who were top of the table.

Hussain M'Barki - a valuable signing from French Rugby Union in 1981.

Right: The programme from Batley versus Fulham. Fulham lost 10-8.

Chapter 10: So near

At the end of March, our final hopes of the Second Division title had disappeared when we were beaten away at York, who went on to win the title. Remarkably, it was Les Sheard, one of the players we had considered buying earlier in the season, who was our undoing. With the score at 10-10 and five minutes to go, Sheard scored a marvellous try to beat us.

However, with the visit of Whitehaven the following Sunday, 5 April 1981, we had a chance to make almost sure of going up in third place behind York and Wigan. A crowd of more than 6,500 saw us turn in probably our most clinical performance of the season. We tore Whitehaven's defence to shreds, scoring five magnificent tries to win 15-0. The only blackspots of the afternoon were a diabolical late tackle by Peter Stoddart that left Mal Aspey concussed and the kicking of Carl Radbone. We were looking for a second string goal kicker and Carl, in practice, kicked very well but he was unable to produce the same form in this particular game. His first match disaster against Rochdale at Fulham must have sapped his confidence. I recognised that it was only inexperience and I was hoping that he would develop in the future.

This win meant that promotion was virtually assured four matches before the end of the season. Whitehaven eventually finished fourth in the table. Now, no matter what Huddersfield, Swinton or Whitehaven did, we only needed a maximum of three points to clinch third place and promotion. The four matches we had to do it in were Batley, Rochdale and Huddersfield, away, and Doncaster at home. It was felt by most people that Huddersfield and Swinton would both drop points and we would possibly need only one win.

At the Batley game, the next week, the pressure began to build up. "Team of the Season", screamed one paper and Frank Clough in the *Sun's* "Opinion" piece said we were the sporting sensation of the season. The players, beginning to tire at the end of a long hard campaign, began to believe everything that was written. They felt they only had to turn up to win. I was not so sure. It was Batley's

Centenary match. Dignitaries from the Rugby League and great players from Batley's past were invited for the grand parade before the game.

Meanwhile, the whole of the Rugby League press seemed to be there... eventually. Many had never been to Batley for years and some found the ground hard to find. Brian Batty of the *Daily Mail* was one. "I got lost, I haven't been here in 20 years," he said, after arriving just before the kick-off. Unfortunately, Brian's journey and that of many others was wasted. We never got into our stride. The eyes of the nation were on us for the second time in a season. But things went horribly wrong. It was a complete contrast to the Wigan match at the start of the campaign.

Batley were so keyed up. They tackled like demons and played well above their normal ability. Our build-up to the match had not been ideal and we were at sixes-and-sevens. For one of the few times in the season, we let ourselves down. Despite leading 8-3 at half-time, by courtesy of four Iain MacCorquodale goals, we could not hold on. In a late rally, Batley snatched a 10-8 victory and the champagne that had been neatly crated in the boot of the team coach, had to go on ice yet again. The disappointment was shattering. The dressing room, which had been expecting to witness a marvellous celebration, instead resembled a morgue.

Everyone knew where we went wrong. Nothing was said. There was nothing to say. Our chance to finish in style had slipped through our fingers and it was a long way home that evening. The jokers were quiet. I was bitterly disappointed but at least we had a chance to redeem ourselves four days later at Rochdale Hornets.

The reaction of the fans was incredible. During the next week, the club received so many phone calls. "Can we still be promoted?" "Have we blown it?" "The soccer club has been so near so many times, you are not going to mess it up, are you?" We assured each one of them that we were determined not to mess it up and that we would win promotion.

It was at this time that we decided to arrange a challenge match on the eve of the Wembley Challenge Cup Final. Every year, as many as

100,000 Rugby League fans travel to London for Rugby League's big match of the year. Many arrive on the Friday before the game the next day. Their entertainment had been limited to expensive shows in London's West End or spending the evening at expensive bars or in their hotels.

I was convinced that if a match could be staged then some of the fans who travel down the day before would be tempted to come and watch. It would be the first time that a game had been staged in London before the final and it would give the supporters the opportunity to visit Craven Cottage - in some cases, for the first time. The only problem was, who would be the opposition. The Cup Final teams were Widnes and Hull Kingston Rovers and it seemed a sensible idea to approach Hull, the deadly rivals of Rovers. We also considered Bradford Northern, who were on course for their second successive Slalom Lager First Division Championship title.

Finally, the choice went to Bradford. They accepted the challenge and, with impeccable timing, claimed the title a couple of weeks later. The match was set: Fulham, Rugby League's success story of the season (or any season) versus the champions for the last two years.

The game caught the imagination of a great number of the supporters. Many of the remaining Cup Final tickets were snapped up by the fans of the game, many from West Yorkshire and particularly Bradford, who had made no plans to travel to Wembley. Our idea to make it a capital Rugby League weekend proved to be a success. Interest in what, on paper, seemed a fascinating Challenge Cup Final, was further enhanced by Fulham, the Second Division team of the year meeting the First Division champions for two years running. Obviously I am not claiming that the Bradford game was the sole reason 94,000 people travelled to Wembley but, because of that night, many previously unsold Cup Final tickets were bought.

However, we still had the little matter of promotion to settle. The match at Rochdale had already been shrouded in a little controversy. The game should have been played on 22 February but heavy snow had meant the game was called off, despite the valiant but ultimately futile efforts to clear the pitch. We were all set for the match to be played on a midweek night.

Instead, Rochdale, obviously hoping for a large crowd, suggested Good Friday. This did not suit us. We had managed to switch a home match against Blackpool to 1 March from Good Friday so that we would not have to play three games in four days at such a vital time during the season, which was the original fixture list. We did not want to recreate that situation.

We suggested several mid-week dates between March and Easter. Rochdale rejected every one and stuck out for Good Friday. In the end, we wrote to the Rugby League to appeal. Luckily for us, there is no way a club can force another to play on Good Friday, but the League ruled the match must be played on the Thursday evening instead.

In a way, this was worse as there would be no papers to report our success on the Friday morning and the fans might have found it difficult to get trains running north because of the holiday period. However, we were stuck with it.

So near - Batley versus Fulham April 1981

Chapter 11: Rochdale and promotion

The Athletic Grounds, Rochdale, was not the most glamorous place in the Rugby League. Deep in terrace-lined Edwardian streets, the stadium had seen better times, but never had there been a more fitting ground for Fulham to clinch promotion.

Rochdale had not exactly welcomed Fulham's move into Rugby League with open arms. Their chairman, Jack Grindrod, had raised several well-meant queries about the scheme before we were admitted to the League. They were the only club to beat us in the League at Craven Cottage. We wanted revenge. No side had completed the double over us and we were determined that honour would not be Rochdale's.

Also, I signed as a professional for Rochdale Hornets in 1949, as a 19-year-old and I had several enjoyable seasons and many fond memories of the Athletic Grounds. I could see no better way of rounding off the historic season than winning promotion there.

Despite the fact it was Maundy Thursday - with no papers next day - there was another large press contingent and even more pleasing was the number of fans who had made the journey to join in the celebrations, because celebrations there were going to be.

As we travelled to Rochdale, the talk by our players was of how to beat the Hornets and by how many points. We were supremely confident. In the dressing room before the game, the laughing and joking was replaced by a steely determination. This time, there were to be no mistakes.

Rochdale were never in with a chance. Aspey, Cambriani and Beverley all scored tries while MacCorquodale kicked four goals and Eckersley, two drop goals. We won 19-5. It was a moment to savour. After all the hard work, a dream had come true. Promotion was clinched. The celebrations were fantastic. The 500 or so fans who made the journey chaired the team off.

Amid scenes of jubilation and hysteria, my mind wandered back to the start of the campaign. I had promised promotion. We had achieved it and the relief was tremendous. It was not a feeling of anti-climax

Adrian Cambriani scoring at Rochdale, leaving Henderson Gill
behind him

Preparing to play Doncaster - Reg Bowden and John Wood
with the team mascot

but a feeling that the worries of the world had been lifted from one's shoulders. The worry of a season, the worry of spending someone else's money, the worry that the fans might not come. All had been vanquished.

I left the players singing in the bath with the champagne that had been waiting five days to be opened, finally flowing. The Rochdale club had catered marvellously for our fans and they were toasting us in no uncertain manner. The rumour was that they almost drank Rochdale dry that night and it is believed that some spent days wandering around the moors trying to find their way back to the M1 motorway.

In contrast to the riotous celebrations by the fans, my drink was much quieter. I slowly sipped a bottle of Blue Bass light ale - it tasted like champagne that night - and reflected on a job well done. The boardroom was strangely subdued. The Rochdale directors slipped away slowly into the night but I was determined to savour the moment.

People said that it could not be done. Promotion, they said, was a wild dream. Fulham were going to be a joke side they claimed. They were all proved wrong. We were in the promotion places all season and with the smallest squad in Rugby League. A squad, for the most part, totalling 18 in number - never more than 22 players.

Never did we field the same team in two consecutive matches. It was a testimony to the quality of players I had acquired - we still managed promotion. To lesser sides, to lesser men, that burden would have been too much.

Finally, in the early hours of the morning, we slipped away - the victors! Everyone in sport will tell you that there is no better feeling than winning. Fulham RLFC that season had been a victory, not only for the players and officials that were involved, but also for the sport of Rugby League.

After two days of revelry and congratulations, the real anti-climax came at Huddersfield. Never can a trip have been more unwelcome. Huddersfield is not the easiest place to win at normally, but after winning promotion, it was hard to raise any enthusiasm. Huddersfield, on the other hand, had to win. They still had an outside chance of promotion if Whitehaven came a "cropper" in their final matches.

We never got going. Huddersfield cruised home 8-3. However, it was still not enough for the Fartown team to gain promotion. Although level on points with the Cumbrians, they needed York to beat Whitehaven by a huge score on the last day of the season. York were never in with a shout and crashed 25-10. Whitehaven were promoted and Huddersfield had to spend another season in the Second Division.

If the Rochdale celebrations had been a rather private affair, the final match at Craven Cottage against Doncaster, was to be the fans' celebration. There could have been no better opposition really. With all respect to Doncaster, who were one place off the bottom of the league, they did not prove too difficult to beat. With a hat-trick of tries by Eckersley, and others by van Bellen, Aspey, Cambriani, Lester, MacCorquodale and Herdman, together with five goals by Corky, we crushed the visitors 37-11 - our highest score and the largest winning margin of the season. The fans enjoyed it tremendously - the leading figures were chaired from the field. Reg Bowden described it afterwards as emotional an occasion as the Wigan match at the start of the campaign.

Not satisfied with chairing the players off the field, the spectators demanded a balcony appearance at the Cottage. With champagne spraying, they cheered wildly.

One player determined not to miss the occasion was Martin Herdman. As he dashed off the field, club chairman Ernie Clay moved to have a few words with the London-born player. Not recognising him, Martin brushed him aside, saying: "Sorry mate, this is my biggest moment and I am not missing it for anything." Ernie was not offended. It was the best day that he had seen at Craven Cottage during his reign as chairman. "Nothing to match it," he claimed.

The players had more to celebrate that evening at the London Tara Hotel, when the club held its inaugural dinner. It was awards time. Players' Player of the Year: David Allen; Fans' Player of the Year: John Wood; Leading try scorer: Mal Aspey; Awards for internationals: Martin Herdman and Adrian Cambriani and for the retiring captain: Tony Karalius.

There was also something for me - a splendid carriage clock. For once in my life, as Reg Bowden was quick to point out, I was speechless. The evening passed well and thoughts began to turn to the Bradford match and yet another night for rejoicing.

The carriage clock Harold Genders received at the end of the 1980-1981 season in recognition of the team's achievements (Photo: Peter Lush)

Harold Genders with Ernie Clay
(Photo courtesy Harold Genders)

Harold Genders holding the 1982-3 Second Division Championship Trophy
(Photo courtesy Harold Genders)

20 years on: Ron Snares (former Supporters Club chairman), Roy
Lester, Harold Genders, Hussain M'Barki and Tony Gourley, after the
London Broncos versus Wigan 20th anniversary match on 25 June 2000.
(photo: Peter Lush)

Fulham RLFC 1980-1981:

Back row: George Noyce (Club Secretary), Tony Kinsey, David Hull, Tony Gourley, Ian van Bellen, John Wood, David Allen, Roy Lester, David Eckersley.
Front row: Malcolm Macdonald (Director), Mal Aspey, Reg Bowden, Ernest Clay (chairman), Tony Karalius, Harold Genders (Director), Derek Noonan, Adrian Cambriani, Colin Welland (Director)

1980 - 1981 mid-season Fulham team group

The 1981 - 1982 Fulham team with Colin Welland, who is holding the Oscar he won for *Chariots of Fire*. The photo is signed: "Thanks for everything Harold. Colin 1983"

The 1982 -1983 Second Division Championship squad. This photo was taken at the start of the 1983 - 1984 season. Hussain M'Barki and Charlie Jones are not in the picture, but two players, John O'Donovan and Gordon Walters are, although they never played for the club. The players: Back: David Hull, Steve Mills, Alan Dearden, Dave Allen, Peter Souto, John O'Donovan, Shaun Hoare, Harry Beverley, Roy Lester, Trevor Stockley, Adrian Cambriani. Middle: Carl Radbone, Gordon Walters, Chris Ganley, Harold Genders, Tony Gourley, Reg Bowden, David Eckersley, Steve Diamond, Steve Bayliss. Front: Tony Kinsey, John Crossley, John Dalgreen, Joe Doherty.

(Photo: Courtesy Harold Genders)

Chapter 12: Reflections

After the magnificent victory against Bradford, the players and their families went on holiday to Ernie Clay's hotel in Portugal. I stayed behind to sign new players to build a team for the challenge of the First Division.

I realised that some of the older players I had signed for the first season promotion campaign had done their job. I felt they would not have the pace for the First Division and would need to be replaced by younger players.

Tony Karalius had done a magnificent job for us, both as hooker and team captain. He had promised to play one season for us. He left and I replaced him in the key role of hooker with John Dalgreen. John had played for Warrington when I was a director there and I knew he was a high quality player although his career had been held back by a serious injury. John was a fiery character and at times had disciplinary problems, but my faith in his quality as a player was shown when he became the only Fulham player ever to be selected for Great Britain when he played against the all-conquering Australian tourists in 1982.

Iain MacCorquodale had been a consistent goal-kicker, but was now reaching the veteran stage. I replaced him with Steve Diamond, who I signed from Wakefield Trinity. Steve was a Welsh international and could play in any of the back positions.

At full-back, we released the veteran John Risman because we had Chris Ganley who played in that position. Steve Diamond could also play full-back.

The other player I released was Ian van Bellen. I had originally signed Ian as a squad player, but he had become the Fulham crowd's hero, with his large frame and balding head, running into the opposition. Unfortunately; I believed he was not now fast enough for the First Division.

Another younger player we signed was John Crossley. He had been a regular try scorer from stand-off in York's successful Second Division campaign and I believed he would give us more attacking options.

Unfortunately we had an injury crisis at the start of the season. This was exacerbated by John Wood, David Hull and Derek Noonan going into dispute with the club just before we played Warrington at home in September. The three players who were in dispute were dropped, although John Wood and David Hull later returned to play for the club.

The players had been in London for a couple of days before the game, filming a television commercial for Grillsteaks, which later became famous throughout the north of England because it featured Rugby League. It was our second advertising venture - the previous season the players had appeared with attractive female topless models on the Vladivar Vodka calendar.

For the Warrington game, a very important one for me given my past involvement with the Wilderspool side, Tony Gourley had to be on the bench despite not being fully fit because of our injury problems. The players responded to the situation magnificently, with Roy Lester - another former Warrington man - having one of his best games for Fulham. We won 28-9.

My policy of signing younger players continued. In September, we signed Shaun Hoare, a 6 foot 5 inches tall forward from Rochdale Hornets. They had been the only team to win at Craven Cottage the previous season and I had been impressed by Shaun. He went on to play 90 games for Fulham, but I feel he never developed to his full potential.

Another exciting recruit was Hussain M'Barki, a Moroccan international Rugby Union winger who was playing in French Rugby Union. It took Hussain time to find his feet in Rugby League, when he joined us in October, but his pace and try-scoring added to our attacking game.

After these signings, I was told that no more money was available for new players. This was a problem because Fulham had made a huge impact on Rugby League in the first season. It was now essential that we establish ourselves in the First Division and not become a 'yo-yo' team - promoted one season, relegated the next. If I had been given the resources to sign top quality First Division players more would

80

have joined us, ensuring a First Division future. As it was, with limited resources, only two of the players I signed then had First Division experience.

We had some good results that season, but injury problems with a small squad caught up with us. The Rugby League authorities did not help. We were fined when we could not field a team at Bradford because of injuries and then had to play at Featherstone four days later with only 14 players. By the end of the season we were borrowing amateurs to be able to field a team, such was our injury crisis. We ended the season being narrowly relegated back to the Second Division. How well we could play was shown with an 11-10 victory at Craven Cottage over champions-elect Leigh towards the end of the season.

The team we had in 1982-3, my third season with Fulham, was, I believe, the best one of my time at the club. This was despite very limited resources being provided for new players. In November 1982, we signed Welsh winger Steve Bayliss from St Helens on loan. He made an immediate impact and scored tries regularly. His permanent transfer was funded by Roy and Barbara Close, who were in discussions with the Clay family at this time about buying the club. They also paid half of the transfer fees for Steve Mills and Charlie Jones, two young players we signed from Widnes to strengthen our squad in March 1983.

One of the highlights of that season was when more than 10,000 people saw us play the Australian tourists at Craven Cottage. We lost 5-22, with Hussain M'Barki scoring our try. We gave them a good game, despite losing Joe Doherty with a nasty injury.

Later that season we were promoted as champions, a victory against York at Craven Cottage confirming the title with two matches still to play.

However, another sign of the growing problems at the club had come towards the end of the season. There were problems with the Craven Cottage pitch and we had a backlog of fixtures. Because the football team were pushing for promotion to the First Division (now the Premier League), it was decided that three of our home games would have to be played elsewhere. Finding a venue in London for two of the games proved to be impossible, partly because professional Rugby League was not allowed to be played on Rugby Union grounds in those days, so the matches against Swinton and Huddersfield had to be played at Widnes. This was a great disappointment to our supporters. The final match of the season was played at Chelsea's Stamford Bridge ground, where we were presented with the Second Division trophy.

But, despite winning promotion again, I was still not given resources to build a team that could compete in the First Division. I felt that promises made in the past had been broken and decided to stay for the first six games to see if any more money for players would be forthcoming. We had signed Alan Dearden, a former Widnes forward who had been out of the game for two years after a serious knee injury, but John Wood had joined Salford in exchange for centre Trevor Stockley.

Unfortunately, the resources I needed were not made available and I had no option but to resign. The match after I had announced my resignation, the team responded magnificently with a 29-24 victory at Craven Cottage over Hull. I remember listening on the radio at home in my garden to how my team were doing, which was a very strange sensation. But my fears were borne out with Fulham being relegated again and, as in the previous First Division campaign having to use amateurs to be able to field a side towards the end of the season.

During my time with the club I never had more than 24 players in the squad at any one time and most of the time less than 22. Ernie Clay had said he had sold footballer Richard Money to Liverpool and bought a Rugby League team. In fact he got change! Looking back, I believe that the question of the future of Craven Cottage and its potential for property development became paramount, ahead of trying to develop the Rugby League club. A couple of years later, Ernie Clay sold his shares in Fulham Football Club to a property developer, putting the future of Craven Cottage as a football ground into question.

The first season had shown the possibilities for Rugby League in London. Had I been given the resources to build a large squad, I believe Fulham could have become a real force in Rugby League. This would have been reflected in increased gates - you have to invest to accumulate. I always knew that the crowds would fall away with a struggling side. The opportunity was missed after the first season, although I am pleased that Rugby League has managed to survive for 20 years in London, including the historic Challenge Cup Final appearance in 1999, which I was pleased to attend.

I was also invited to the London Broncos match against Wigan in June 2000 when the club marked the 20th anniversary. I enjoyed the day and it was good to meet players and supporters from my time at the club.

Twenty years on: London Broncos versus Wigan 25 June 2000 Super League match at The Valley. The Broncos played in a replica of the original Fulham kit. Despite this they lost 12-16.

Dominic Peters watches Kris Radlinski being tackled. Dominic was the first London born player to come through the club's academy scheme and win a regular first team place. (Photo: Peter Lush)

Top: Broncos' forward Justin Dooley on the charge at Terry O'Connor
Bottom: The main stand at The Valley (photos: Peter Lush)

Appendices

Appendix 1: 1980-1981 Match reports and teams

September

14th Wigan home 24-5

A perfect day. A side recruited in eight weeks beat one of the all-time great clubs 24-5. Even more incredible was the supportive and widespread press reaction. Fulham could not have dreamed of a better start. An early goal by MacCorquodale put Fulham ahead, and the nerves were really settled by two Cambriani tries before half-time. Second-half tries by Tuffs and Allen sealed an unbelievable debut.

Fulham: Risman, Cambriani, Aspey, Noonan, MacCorquodale, Eckersley, Bowden, van Bellen, Karalius, Lester, Gourley, Allen, Hull. Subs: Tuffs, Wood. *Tries:* Cambriani (2), Tuffs (2), Allen. *Goals:* MacCorquodale (4). *Drop-goal:* Eckersley.

Wigan: Fairbairn, Ramsdale, Willicombe, Davies, Hornby, Coyle, Flowers, Townend, Pendlebury, Smith, Clough, Hollingsworth, Boyd. Subs: Bolton, Melling. *Try:* Coyle. *Goal:* Fairbairn.

21st Keighley away 13-24

After the action the reaction. Fulham fell flat against a pumped up home side. Fulham were in front at half-time 13-9 with tries by Aspey (2) and Tuffs, but ran out of steam and ideas and crumbled to defeat. Reg Bowden commented that: "After being on Cloud Nine all week we have come down to earth with a real bang... the crowd certainly lifted Keighley once they realised their side had a chance of winning." Harry Beverley made his debut.

Keighley: Jickells, Moll, Clark, Rowett, Beale, Bardgett, Diabira, Sellers, Raistrick, Banham, Farrell, Clarkson, Garner. Subs: North, Hawksworth. *Tries:* Jickells, Moll, Clark, Bardgett, Garner. *Goals:* Bardgett (4). *Drop-goal:* Banham.

Fulham: Risman, Cambriani, Aspey, Noonan, MacCorquodale, Tuffs, Bowden, van Bellen, Karalius, Beverley, Wood, Lester, Allen. Subs: Kinsey, Hull. *Tries:* Aspey (2), Tuffs. *Goals:* MacCorquodale (2).

28th Swinton home 25-11

The season got back on track in front of healthy crowd of 5,589. An early try by Derek Noonan put Fulham in control all day against a game Swinton side. Wood and Eckersley scored further tries before half-time. Three more tries by Karalius, Aspey and Cambriani sealed a comfortable win, the

Welshman sprinting 60 yards to score in the final minute and earning a standing ovation. Tony Kinsey made his debut, coming on as a substitute for Neil Tuffs.

Fulham: Eckersley, Cambriani, Noonan, Aspey, MacCorquodale, Tuffs, Bowden, van Bellen, Karalius, Lester, Wood, Gourley, Hull. Subs: Kinsey, Allen. *Tries:* Eckersley, Cambriani, Noonan, Aspey, Karalius, Wood. *Goals:* MacCorquodale (3). Drop-goal; Eckersley.

Swinton: Gorton, Drummond, Bruen, Graham, Carsley, Wilson, Taylor, Earl, Middlehurst, Ashcroft, Grice, Nicholson, Peters. Subs: Derbyshire, Cooper. *Tries:* Drummond, Graham, Carsley. *Goal:* Gorton.

October

5th Blackpool Borough away 15-2

A good defensive performance against the lowly Seasiders as Fulham achieved their first away win. In a tight game Bowden and Kinsey scored tries with four goals and a drop-goal from MacCorquodale completing a decisive victory.

Blackpool Borough: Oldham, Chester, Bailey, Heritage, Oxley, Arnold, Green, Gamble, Parry, Waterworth, Holmes, Frodsham, Corcoran. Subs: Tilly, Earle. *Goal:* Oxley.

Fulham: Allen, Cambriani, Noonan, Risman, MacCorquodale, Kinsey, Bowden, Beverley, Karalius, Lester, Gourley, Wood, Hull. Subs: Aspey, van Bellen. *Tries:* Kinsey, Bowden. *Goals:* MacCorquodale (4). *Drop-goal:* MacCorquodale.

12th Huddersfield home 30-7

The side went into top gear against a much fancied Fartown outfit. Once again Derek Noonan scored an early try and a further John Risman score put the Londoners 15-7 up at half-time. The second half was a cake walk with further tries from with Gourley and Bowden. MacCorquodale scored a try, seven goals and a drop-goal for a Fulham record 18 points in a match.

Fulham: Allen, Risman, Noonan, Aspey, MacCorquodale, Kinsey, Bowden, Beverley, Karalius, van Bellen, Gourley, Wood, Hull. Subs: Eckersley, Lester. *Tries:* Risman, Noonan, MacCorquodale, Bowden, Gourley. *Goals:* MacCorquodale (7). *Drop-goals:* MacCorquodale.

Huddersfield: Knight, Cramp, Leathley, Barton, Hirst, Denton, Bates, Johnson, Wroe, Lyons, Wood, Halmshaw, Branch. Subs: Cyrus, McHugh. *Try:* Denton. *Goals:* Hirst (2).

19th Doncaster away 28-16

Fulham established an early lead against perennial strugglers Doncaster at Tattersfield before a small crowd of 628. The Londoners managed three tries before half-time from Ganley, Aspey and a rare score from Ian van Bellen. Once again it was MacCorquodale who won the game with two tries and five goals. Chris Ganley and Graham Worgan made their debuts.

Doncaster: Healey, Noble, Buckton, Hartley, K. Millet, Brook, Paterson, G. Ellis, Knott, K. Ellis, Perigo, Matthews, Davies. Subs: Piper, Hossell. *Tries:* Paterson (2). *Goals:* Noble (5).

Fulham: Ganley, Cambriani, Risman, Worgan, MacCorquodale, Aspey, Bowden, Beverley, Karalius, van Bellen, Allen, Wood, Hull. Subs: Kinsey, Gourley. *Tries:* MacCorquodale (2), Ganley, Aspey, Karalius, van Bellen. *Goals:* MacCorquodale (5).

26th York home 23-5

This was an important game as York were also battling for promotion. In a tight first half John Wood scored the only home try to edge Fulham in front 7-5. In the second half Fulham had all the right ideas as tries by Aspey, Noonan and Eckersley saw the men in black comfortably home. This was an important win for the promotion push in front of 7,179 happy Londoners. Fulham had now won six out of the first seven league games. One unwanted note was Roy Lester being the first Fulham player to be sent off when he was dismissed five minutes from full-time.

Fulham: Ganley, Cambriani, Aspey, Noonan, MacCorquodale, Eckersley, Bowden, Beverley, Karalius, van Bellen, Gourley, Wood, Hull. Subs: Kinsey, Lester. *Tries:* Eckersley, Aspey, Noonan, Wood. *Goals:* MacCorquodale (5). Drop-goal: Eckersley.

York: Smith, Morgan, Sheard, Brown, Gibson, Crossley, Inns, Wardell, Maskill, Dunkerley, White, Price, McDermott. Subs: Hagan, Kirkbride. *Try:* Crossley. *Drop-goals:* Inns, Price.

November

9th Bramley home 10-7

Fulham struggled against the mid-table Villagers. First-half tries by Cambriani and Eckersley saw them comfortably in front 8-0. The second half was forgettable as the Yorkshiremen refused to buckle and Fulham were happy to win 10-7. Welsh recruit from Rugby Union, Peter Souto, made his debut as a second-half substitute.

Fulham: Risman, Cambriani, Noonan, Worgan, MacCorquodale, Eckersley, Bowden, Beverley, Karalius, van Bellen, Allen, Wood, Hull. Subs: Aspey, Souto. *Tries:* Cambriani, Eckersley. *Goals:* MacCorquodale (2).

Bramley: Bibb, Dyes, Nicholson, Winterbottom, Francis, Ayres, Langton, Grinhaff, Tennant, Burke, Knowles, Huddlestone, Bond. Subs: Johnston, Bowman. *Try:* Tennant. *Goals:* Bibb (2).

16th Dewsbury away 9-7

Another win ground out by Fulham. Iain MacCorquodale scored all the points with a try and three goals in the first half. The second half was dominated by Dewsbury but the Londoners held out 9-7 to record a seventh straight win.

Dewsbury: Richardson, Dunford, Austin, Agar, Lowe, Watson, Lee, Briggs, Dufton, King, Wood, Watkins, Crossley. Subs: Cummins, Broadhead. *Try:* Lee. *Goals:* Agar (2).

Fulham: Risman, Cambriani, Aspey, Noonan, MacCorquodale, Eckersley, Bowden, Beverley, Kinsey, van Bellen, Gourley, Allen, Hull. Subs: Karalius, Souto. *Try:* MacCorquodale. *Goals:* MacCorquodale (3).

23rd Leeds home 9-3 John Player Trophy round one

A big game, a big win and a big crowd of 12,583. Once again the Fulham defence was magnificent, with First Division Leeds's only try coming in the 72nd minute. The boot won the game for Fulham with two goals from MacCorquodale and two drop-goals plus the only try from David Eckersley. This game proved that the win against Wigan was no freak and served notice to the big clubs that Fulham were becoming a force to be reckoned with. Victory was achieved despite Reg Bowden being injured and missing most of the second half. Bowden said that the performance was "absolutely magnificent".

Fulham: Risman, Cambriani, Aspey, Noonan, MacCorquodale, Eckersley, Bowden, Beverley, Karalius, Gourley, Wood, Allen, Hull. Subs: Kinsey, van Bellen. *Try:* Eckersley. *Goals:* MacCorquodale (2). *Drop-goals:* Eckersley (2).

Leeds: Oulton, Smith, Heselwood, Hague, Atkinson, Holmes, Dick, Harrison, Miller, Pitchford, Eccles, Cookson, Heron. Subs: Fletcher, Carroll. *Try:* Eccles.

30th Wigan away 2-15

Back down to earth. The Riversiders were clearly intent on gaining revenge for their defeat at the Cottage. Fulham were not really at the races as Wigan's biggest crowd of the season roared the home team on. A fourth-minute penalty was all Fulham had to show for their efforts in a 15-2 defeat. Ian van Bellen was harshly sent off in the second half. Reg Bowden missed a Fulham game for the first time.

Wigan: Fairbairn, Ramsdale, Butler, Ratcliffe, Stockley, Bolton, Stephens, O'Neill, Williams, Bowman, Boyd, Campbell, Pendlebury. Subs: Walsh, Hollingsworth. *Tries:* Ramsdale, Stockley, Bolton, *Goals:* Pendlebury (2), Fairbairn.

Fulham: Risman, Cambriani, Aspey, Noonan, MacCorquodale, Eckersley, Kinsey, van Bellen, Karalius, Lester, Wood, Gourley, Allen. Subs: Tuffs and Souto. *Goal:* MacCorquodale.

December

7th Leigh away 9-17 John Player Trophy round two

This was the third big game in a row. Fulham's mettle was tested and in a tight game the First Division side had the whip hand and were 7-0 in front at half-time. A better second half performance was not enough, despite a try by Chris Ganley, and Fulham went out of the cup in front of 7,606 spectators.

Leigh: Hogan, Drummond, Bilsbury, Donlan, Fox, Woods, Green, Pyke, Wall, Cooke, Tabern, Platt, Gittins. Subs: Fairhurst, Hobson. *Tries:* Woods, Platt. *Goals:* Woods (5). *Drop-goal:* Fairhurst.

Fulham: Ganley, Cambriani, Aspey, Risman, MacCorquodale, Eckersley, Bowden, Beverley, Karalius, Gourley, Wood, Allen, Hull. Subs: Kinsey and Lester. *Try:* Ganley. *Goals:* MacCorquodale (3).

21st Hunslet home 19-5

Fulham got the season back on track against a battling Hunslet side. Two early tries by Mal Aspey and David Allen, playing at full-back, saw Fulham 7-5 ahead at half-time. The second half was won on cruise control as Fulham's first hat trick of tries - by Cambriani - secured a comfortable Londoners' win.

Fulham: Allen, Cambriani, Aspey, Ganley, MacCorquodale, Eckersley, Bowden, Beverley, Kinsey, van Bellen, Wood, Souto, Hull. Subs: Risman and Lester. *Tries:* Cambriani (3), Aspey, Allen. *Goals:* MacCorquodale (2).

Hunslet: M. Nicholson, Walker, Briers, Smith, I. Nicholson, Lane, King, Windmill, Netzler, Wright, Raybould, Griffiths, Hughes. Subs: Booth, Burgess. *Try:* I. Nicholson. *Goal:* Walker.

28th Batley home 15-5

Another first-half struggle with a lone try from Chris Ganley, playing at centre, and a MacCorquodale penalty gave Fulham a 5-3 half-time lead. The game was won with tries from Roy Lester, playing an unfamiliar role at hooker, and John Wood. The defence was supreme as the Mount Pleasant side went down to defeat. Martin Herdman, the club's first Londoner, and Carl Radbone, the club's third Welsh Rugby Union signing, made their debuts.

Fulham: Risman, Cambriani, Ganley, Radbone, MacCorquodale, Eckersley, Bowden, Beverley, Lester, van Bellen, Wood, Herdman, Kinsey. Subs: Allen and Souto. *Tries:* Ganley, Lester, Wood. *Goals:* MacCorquodale (3).

Batley: Parker, Ratcliffe, Presley, Jones, Oulton, Briggs, Pickerill, Frain, Cummins, Woodall, Watts, Vodden, Rippon. Subs: Piwinski, Watts. *Try:* Jones. *Goal:* Oulton.

January

4th Whitehaven away 0-6

It was not a very happy start to the new year, with a narrow defeat against promotion rivals before a large crowd of 4,235 in the small Cumbrian town. Fulham conceded the only try in the 16th minute and for the rest of the game were unable to break down the home side. Fulham were 'nilled' for the first time.

Whitehaven: Dutton, McClure, Larder, Stoddart, Bulman, O'Neill, Walker, Calvin, Doran, Rae, Martin, Hartley, Thompson. Subs: Huddart, Rose. *Try:* Doran. *Goal:* Dutton. *Drop-goal:* Dutton.

Fulham: Ganley, Cambriani, Aspey, Risman, MacCorquodale, Eckersley, Bowden, Beverley, Kinsey, Lester, Wood, Allen, Hull. Subs: Tuffs, Herdman.

11th Rochdale Hornets home 8-24

There were more worries for Fulham as Rochdale became the first away side to win at the Cottage. The Hornets were 10-0 up after nine minutes and built a 20-3 half time lead, with only a Ganley try for the home side. The second half was not much better for Fulham with only a consolation try from Harry Beverley as the Londoners went down 24-8 and got a real wake-up call for the rest of the season. Two of the Hornets' tries had come from interceptions. Incidentally, Rochdale were the only side that season to travel to the game the day before, rather than on the day of the match.

Fulham: Risman, Cambriani, Ganley, Radbone, MacCorquodale, Eckersley, Bowden, Beverley, Karalius, Lester, Allen, Souto, Hull. Subs: Tuffs and Herdman. *Tries:* Ganley, Beverley. *Goal:* MacCorquodale.
Rochdale Hornets: Grimes, Holland, McGiffen, Gilmore, Gill, Price, Sanderson, Glover, Langan, Gorvin, Hoare, Turley, Coates. Subs: Fletcher, Lowe. *Tries:* Gilmore (2), Gill, Gorvin. *Goals:* Turley (5). *Drop-goal:* Turley.

18th Bramley away 21-11

The club's first double and a much needed win after two defeats. Still the Cottagers did not have it all their own way, being only 10-9 in front at half time. It was MacCorquodale's kicking that was the difference between the sides. Graham Moss made his debut for Fulham.
Bramley: Bibb, Dyes, Winterbottom, K. Olbison, Lund, A. Olbison, Wandless, Grinhaff, Woolford, Bowman, Huddlestone, Burke, Bond. Subs: Hepworth, Tennant. *Tries:* Lund, Wandless, Bowman. *Goal:* Wandless.
Fulham: Ganley, Cambriani, Aspey, Allen, MacCorquodale, Eckersley, Bowden, Beverley, Moss, van Bellen, Gourley, Wood, Hull. Subs: Tuffs, Karalius. *Tries:* Ganley (2), Eckersley, Bowden. *Goals:* MacCorquodale (4). *Drop-goal:* MacCorquodale

25th Huyton home 25-4

Fulham did not concede a try in an emphatic victory, as the lowly Merseysiders managed only two goals. Eckersley deputised for MacCorquodale as goal-kicker and kicked five goals for Fulham. Carl Radbone scored his first try for Fulham in an easy win. A crowd of 5,805 enjoyed the match, showing how the crowds had held up, even against lowly opposition.
Fulham: Ganley, Cambriani, Tuffs, Risman, Radbone, Eckersley, Bowden, van Bellen, Moss, Lester, Gourley, Herdman, Kinsey. Subs: Aspey, Souto. *Tries:* Ganley, Radbone, van Bellen (2), Aspey. *Goals:* Eckersley (5).
Huyton: Tabern, Fitzsimmons, Hunter, Jackson, Leatherbarrow, Corwell, Bishop, Fletcher, Andrews, Middlehurst, Coop, Cooper, Hartley. Subs: Prescott, Goulding. *Goals:* Tabern (2).

February

1st Hunslet away 12-11

This was a nail biter. Fulham found themselves 6-3 down at half time, having scored through a Mal Aspey try. The side dug deep in the second period and a second Aspey try, with a try and goal from MacCorquodale saw the Londoners narrowly scrape home. David Eckersley's drop-goal six minutes from time clinched the win.

Hunslet: Briers, Walker, Muscroft, Booth, I. Nicholson, Lane, King, Raybould, Gibson, Netzler, Griffiths, McGregor, Cooper. Subs: Sykes, Hirst. *Tries:* Lane (2). *Goals:* Walker (2). *Drop-goal:* Cooper.

Fulham: Ganley, Cambriani, Aspey, Allen, MacCorquodale, Eckersley, Bowden, Beverley, Karalius, van Bellen, Gourley, Wood, Hull. Subs: Kinsey, Lester. *Tries:* Aspey (2), MacCorquodale. *Goal:* MacCorquodale. *Drop-goal:* Eckersley.

8th Swinton away 9-13

In front of Swinton's largest crowd of the season the home side pulled off a win that kept their own promotion hopes alive. An early try by Adrian Cambriani was Fulham's only reward as the home team were in front 10-4 at half time. A second-half Ganley try was not enough as Fulham slipped to defeat.

Swinton: Gorton, Vigo, Bruen, Wilson, Drummond, Rutens, Taylor, Grice, Derbyshire, Ashcroft, Clough, Cooper, Peters. Subs: Mellor, Nicholson. *Tries:* Wilson, Drummond, Clough. *Goals:* Gorton (2).

Fulham: Ganley, Cambriani, Aspey, Allen, MacCorquodale, Eckersley, Bowden, Beverley, Karalius, Lester, Gourley, Wood, Hull. Subs: Risman, Herdman. *Tries:* Ganley, Cambriani. *Goal:* MacCorquodale. *Drop-goal:* Eckersley.

15th Wakefield Trinity home 5-9 Challenge Cup round one

Fulham's biggest crowd of 15,013 did not witness another giant killing act. In a tight game, the visitors settled first with a Keith Smith try and they controlled the first half. Fulham improved after the break, but it was only in the latter stages that they came to grips with the First Division side with a David Hull try. But it was too late as the Yorkshire side went through. Iain MacCorquodale received an award marking 2,000 career points in Rugby League before the kick-off.

Fulham: Ganley, Cambriani, Aspey, Noonan, MacCorquodale, Eckersley, Bowden, Beverley, Karalius, van Bellen, Gourley, Allen, Hull. Subs: Risman, Wood. *Try:* Hull. *Goal:* MacCorquodale.

Wakefield Trinity: Box, Fletcher, Day, Smith, Juliff, Topliss, Agar, Murray, McCurrie, Bratt, Thompson, Rayne, Lampowski. Subs: Diamond, Kelly. *Tries:* Smith, Fletcher. *Goal:* Diamond. *Drop-goal:* Agar.

March

1st Blackpool home 8-0

This was a must win game. The Seasiders were very competitive and Fulham were made to fight all the way. Tries by Aspey and Radbone saw a crucial victory assured before 4,715, the lowest crowd of the season. This was the first time Fulham 'nilled' the opposition. New signing Joe Doherty made his debut.

Fulham: Risman, Radbone, Noonan, Aspey, MacCorquodale, Kinsey, Bowden, Lester, Doherty, Gourley, Herdman, Allen, Hull. Subs: Eckersley, Souto. *Tries:* Radbone, Aspey. *Goal:* MacCorquodale.

Blackpool Borough: Charlton, Oxley, Sivori, Tilly, Myers, Bailey, Chester, Gamble, Waterworth, Lomax, Webb, Lyon, Corcoran. Subs: Roberts, Wynyard.

8th Keighley home 24-3

This match brought sweet revenge for the Londoners. It was a comfortable win against Keighley who had inflicted the club's first defeat back in September. Six tries, including two from Mal Aspey gave Fulham a decisive victory.

Fulham: Ganley, Cambriani, Aspey, Noonan, Radbone, Eckersley, Bowden, Beverley, Doherty, Wood, Herdman, Allen, Hull. Subs: Kinsey, Souto. *Tries:* Aspey (2), Cambriani, Herdman, Allen, Souto. *Goals:* Radbone (3).

Keighley: Jickells, Moll, Greenwood, Rowett, Beale, Bardgett, North, Sellers, Hodgson, Farrell, Clarkson, Dickens, Hawksworth. Subs: Wilkes, Moorby. *Try:* Beale.

15th Huyton away 19-3

A comfortable win in front of a tiny crowd of 400 at Alt Park. Three first-half tries from Risman, MacCorquodale and Hull were matched by second-half efforts from Aspey and Lester. Fulham recorded a double against the bottom side, despite missing some of the team's leading players.

Huyton: Tabern, Corwell, Hunter, Fitzpatrick, Jackson, Irwin, Prescott, Fletcher, Andrews, Banham, Saxby, Cooper, Middlehurst. Subs: Bishop, Goulding. *Try:* Hunter.

Fulham: Allen, Risman, Aspey, Tuffs, MacCorquodale, Eckersley, Kinsey, van Bellen, Karalius, Lester, Wood, Souto, Hull. Subs: Doherty, Gourley. *Tries:* Risman, Aspey, Eckersley, Lester, Hull. *Goals:* MacCorquodale (2).

22nd Dewsbury home 16-4

A comfortable win - Fulham's 17th out of 22 Second Division matches. In a tight first half all Fulham had to show was a converted try by Cambriani. The second half was easier, with tries by Noonan, Eckersley and Wood against two goals for the Yorkshire side.

Fulham: Risman, Cambriani, Tuffs, Noonan, MacCorquodale, Eckersley, Kinsey, Beverley, Karalius, van Bellen, Wood, Gourley, Allen. Subs: Bowden, Lester. *Tries:* Cambriani, Noonan, Eckersley, Wood. *Goals:* MacCorquodale (2).

Dewsbury: Richardson, Dunford, Collins, Lowe, Wilson, Hughes, Lee, Mason, Catlin, Long, Wood, Artis, Craven. Subs: Dunford, Brunt. *Goals:* Dunford (2).

29th York away 10-15

A crucial game against the eventual Second Division champions. The high-flying Wasps needed this win to stay top and had their highest home crowd for the season of 7,351. Again it was Welshman Cambriani who was first out of the traps with a try, but later Fulham trailed 10-3. The Londoners fought back to 10-all with a David Allen try, but it was not enough as York edged it 15-10 with a try five minutes from time. David Hull was sent off for Fulham after 58 minutes.

York: Midgley, Pryce, Sheard, Redford, Morgan, Crossley, Harkin, Wardell, Phillippo, Dunkerley, White, Adams, McDermott. Subs: Inns, Kirkbride. *Tries:* Harkin (2), Sheard. *Goals:* Morgan (3)

Fulham: Ganley, Cambriani, Aspey, Noonan, MacCorquodale, Allen, Bowden, Beverley, Doherty, Lester, Wood, Herdman, Hull. Subs: Tuffs, Gourley. *Tries:* Cambriani, Allen. *Goals:* MacCorquodale (2).

April

5th Whitehaven home 15-0

This was another vital game against promotion rivals Whitehaven. In a tense match Fulham were always in control and three first-half tries by Aspey, Eckersley and Bowden set the Londoners on their way. A further try from Eckersley and a late try by John Risman clinched a vital victory and put promotion firmly on the agenda. Only nervous kicking from Carl Radbone prevented a bigger victory. This was the second time Fulham had 'nilled' the opposition.

Fulham: Ganley, Cambriani, Aspey, Tuffs, Radbone, Eckersley, Bowden, van Bellen, Karalius, Gourley, Herdman, Allen, Hull. Subs: Risman, Lester. *Tries:* Eckersley (2), Aspey, Bowden, Risman.

Whitehaven: Dutton, McClure, Larder, Stoddart, Bulman, Walker, Hall, Calvin, Barwise, Grimes, Cottier, Huddart, Thompson. Subs: Rose, Martin.

12ᵗʰ Batley away 8-10

If Fulham won this match the club would be promoted. But the home side in its centenary match was spurred on by their largest crowd of the season and pulled off a shock victory. Batley scored the only try of the game late on and pinched it 10-8. Fulham had to wait for promotion. Reg Bowden admitted that underdogs Batley were "well worth their victory".

Batley: Parker, Presley, Shaw, Jones, Oulton, Briggs, Pickerill, Waltham, Cummins, Woodall, Vodden, Allen, Rippon. Subs: Watts, Frain. *Try:* Briggs. *Goals:* Oulton (3). *Drop-goal:* Oulton.

Fulham: Ganley, Radbone, Risman, Noonan, MacCorquodale, Eckersley, Bowden, Beverley, Doherty, Gourley, Wood, Souto, Kinsey. Subs: Herdman, van Bellen. *Goals:* MacCorquodale (4).

16ᵗʰ Rochdale away 19-5

Fulham were in a hurry to go up and stormed into a 13-4 lead by half time. Tries by Cambriani, Aspey and Beverley secured promotion two games from the end of the season in front of many vociferous Fulham supporters despite the match being played on Maundy Thursday night.

Rochdale Hornets: Grimes, Holland, Price, Gilmore, Gill, Nolan, Sanderson, Breheny, Langan, Glover, Gorvin, Garside, Turley. Subs: Fletcher, Coates. *Goals:* Turley (2). *Drop-goal:* Turley.

Fulham: Ganley, Cambriani, Aspey, Noonan, MacCorquodale, Eckersley, Bowden, Beverley, Karalius, Gourley, Lester, Wood, Hull. Subs: Tuffs, Herdman. *Tries:* Cambriani, Aspey, Beverley. *Goals:* MacCorquodale (4). *Drop-goals:* Eckersley (2).

19ᵗʰ Huddersfield away 3-8

A tough game against the promotion chasing Fartown side, especially after a vital game at Rochdale three days before. The Londoners were edged out, with their points coming from a MacCorquodale penalty and an Eckersley drop-goal.

Huddersfield: Barton, Cramp, Leathley, Slater, Swale, Knight, Bates, Johnson, Clarke, Lyons, McHugh, Johnson, Punter. Subs: Pritchard, Chester. *Try:* Swale. *Goal:* Swale. *Drop-goals:* Swale (2), Knight.

Fulham: Ganley, Cambriani, Noonan, Tuffs, MacCorquodale, Eckersley, Bowden, van Bellen, Doherty, Gourley, Herdman, Hull, Kinsey. Subs: Aspey, Lester. *Goal:* MacCorquodale. *Drop-goal:* Eckersley.

20th Doncaster home 37-11

A day after the Huddersfield defeat, Fulham celebrated promotion by scoring a record 37 points against the lowly Dons. An Eckersley hat-trick plus six more tries made it a satisfactory victory. The club ended the season in third place. Iain MacCorquodale scored a try and five goals as a crowd of 5,849 were able to praise their heroes for achieving promotion at the first attempt. As Reg Bowden said: "A marvellous way to end a marvellous season for the club".

Fulham: Ganley, Cambriani, Aspey, MacCorquodale, Radbone, Eckersley, Bowden, van Bellen, Karalius, Gourley, Lester, Wood, Hull. Subs: Kinsey, Herdman. *Tries:* Eckersley (3), Cambriani, Aspey, MacCorquodale, van Bellen, Lester, Herdman. *Goals:* MacCorquodale (5).

Doncaster: Brook, Piper, Wilson, Noble, K. Millet, Buckton, Finnerty, Perigo, Knott, Ellis, Matthews, Hodgson, Davies. Subs: Harrison, I. Millet. *Tries:* Buckton (3). *Goal:* Noble.

May

1st Bradford Northern home Challenge Match 20-8

This game was set up as a challenge match with well organised publicity, apparently for a £5,000 prize (see appendix 3). The game attracted the London public and northern visitors in town for the next day's Challenge Cup final with 11,926 attending. Fulham were up for it with David Allen scoring four tries, matched by Iain MacCorquodale's four goals, as the Yorkshiremen were defeated. It was a triumphant end to the season. Carwyn James's report in *The Guardian* said that: "The Fulham supporters have done the club proud and it is now up to Colin Welland and his fellow directors to put their money where their mouths are. Otherwise the First Division may be a short and eventually a return journey for Fulham". Prophetic words indeed.

Fulham: Ganley, Cambriani, Aspey, Risman, MacCorquodale, Eckersley, Bowden, Beverley, Karalius, van Bellen, Gourley, Allen, Hull. Subs: Tuffs, Doherty. *Tries:* Allen (4). *Goals:* MacCorquodale (4).

Bradford Northern: Mumby, Barends, A. Parker, D. Parker, Grant, Stephenson, Redfearn, Thompson, Handforth, Fidler, Grayshon, Jackson, Idle. Subs: Ferres, Trotter. *Tries:* D. Parker, Ferres. *Goal:* Mumby.

Appendix 2: The 1980-1981 Players

Dave Allen

One of the club's six signings from Widnes, Dave could play equally well in the pack or at centre. He joined Widnes in 1972 from Rugby Union and won Lancashire representative honours in Rugby League. A regular try scorer, he left Fulham in 1984 to join Reg Bowden at Warrington.

Mal Aspey

Mal joined Widnes in 1963. A 6 foot tall centre, his experience was crucial for Fulham in the battle for promotion. He had made over 500 appearances for Widnes including three Challenge Cup finals and was given a testimonial. He left Fulham in 1982 to join Wigan.

Harry Beverley

Harry was signed from Workington Town just before the first match and completed the initial Fulham squad. He was a powerful prop forward. Harry's Rugby League career started with Leeds in 1968. He then played for Dewsbury for seven years, including being a member of their 1973 championship winning team, and joined Workington in 1978. He won one England cap. He played for four seasons at Fulham, making over 100 appearances. After leaving Fulham, he played a few games for Carlisle and Workington.

Reg Bowden

Player/coach and scrum-half, Reg was one of the key figures at the club in the Craven Cottage era. He signed for Widnes in 1968 and was a major influence in the Widnes teams that dominated Rugby League in the 1970s. He made 16 major cup final appearances for Widnes, including four Wembley cup finals and won every club honour in the game. After leaving Fulham in June 1984 he was coach at Warrington for two years.

Adrian Cambriani

The club's first signing from Rugby Union, Adrian was a Welsh Rugby Union Youth and Schools International. His youth, speed and good looks attracted a great deal of publicity for Fulham. He played on the right wing and made over 100 appearances for the club, before retiring in 1987. He won three Welsh caps. Injuries prevented him fulfilling the potential he showed as a young player but he made an important contribution to establishing Rugby League at Fulham.

Joe Doherty

Joe was signed from Rochdale Hornets in March 1981, having spent a month on loan at Fulham. He had previously played for Warrington and Widnes. He played at hooker and was signed as cover for Tony Karalius, but could also play in the second row or at loose forward. He made his debut against Blackpool on 1 March 1981 and went on to make over 100 appearances for Fulham before retiring at the end of the 1984-85 season.

David Eckersley

David was another important signing for Fulham. He turned professional for Leigh and played for them in their 1971 Challenge Cup Final victory. In 1972 he moved to St Helens and in 1976 to Widnes, winning many honours including another Challenge Cup winners medal in 1979. In international Rugby League, he won four Great Britain and five England caps. He mainly played at stand off for Fulham, but had played much of his career at full back. He was a regular drop-goal scorer. He left the club in 1984, having made 93 appearances for Fulham.

Chris Ganley

Chris was signed by Fulham from Warrington in October 1980. He mainly played at full back and made 60 appearances for Fulham before leaving at the end of the 1983-4 season. He had a short loan spell at St Helens in 1983-4. He later played for Blackpool Borough and then Springfield Borough when the club moved to Wigan.

Tony Gourley

Tony's Rugby League career started with his home town club, Rochdale Hornets. A well built forward, he won Lancashire representative honours while at Rochdale and then played two seasons for Salford before joining Fulham. He became club captain in the club's second season and played for Fulham until retiring through injury in 1985, having made over 100 appearances for the club.

Martin Herdman

Martin Herdman was the team's first Londoner. He had played Rugby Union and was an accomplished amateur boxer before joining Fulham. He gained some experience in amateur Rugby League before signing professional and making his debut in December 1980. He was a fast running back row forward who developed very well in his time at the club, including winning Welsh international honours. He left the club at the end of the 1983-4 season but returned to play a handful of games when the club was based at Chiswick. While playing for Fulham he also did some professional boxing, and when he left had trials for the Kansas City Chiefs American Football team.

David Hull

David was another quality signing for Fulham from Widnes, mainly playing at loose forward. He had top flight experience with Widnes and St Helens. He made Challenge Cup final appearances for both clubs. He did not play for Fulham in 1981-2 or 1982-3, but returned to make 24 appearances in 1983-4, before leaving the club at the end of that season.

Tony Karalius

Tony was recruited by Fulham from Wigan, and had been considering retirement before being persuaded to play one more season in the key role of hooker. He was also the team captain. A member of a famous Rugby League family, he won five Great Britain caps and was a member of the victorious 1972 World Cup squad. He played for St Helens in their Wembley Challenge Cup Final victory against Widnes in 1976. He also played for Widnes and after leaving Fulham helped launch another new Rugby League club by playing a further season for the Cardiff Blue Dragons.

Tony Kinsey

Tony turned professional with Fulham, although his Rugby League career started at Widnes as an amateur. He was a versatile player and a valuable member of the squad. He was a popular player with the club's fans and made over 150 appearances for the club, finally leaving in 1986 to join Huddersfield. Possibly his best position was loose forward, but he could also play at scrum half, stand off or hooker with equal skill and commitment.

Roy Lester

Roy was the first player to sign for Fulham. He had previously played for Leigh and Warrington and was an important addition to the Fulham pack. Injury restricted his appearances in his third and fourth seasons at the club. He became assistant coach in 1983-4 and then in 1984-85 became coach after Reg Bowden joined Warrington and the club left Craven Cottage. His commitment to the club through difficult times in 1984-85 and 1985-86 is fondly remembered by the supporters and he played a crucial role in keeping the club alive at that time. He left in 1986 when new owners decided to base the team in the south. He subsequently became coach at Carlisle and then assistant coach at Warrington until the start of Super League, when business interests prevented him being able to work full time in Rugby League, which the new competition would have required.

Iain MacCorquodale

Iain first played Rugby League for Salford and then in 1972 joined Workington. In 1977-78 he broke the Workington points record for a season with 306. He was a reliable goalkicker and usually played on the wing. During his season with Fulham he was given an award for achieving 2,000 points in professional Rugby League. After leaving Fulham at the end of the first season he joined Blackpool Borough.

Graham Moss

Graham was a hooker from the Springfield amateur club who played a couple of games on trial in January 1981. He did not join the club on a permanent basis.

Derek Noonan

Derek added quality to Fulham's backs in the first season. He was signed from St Helens and had previously played for Warrington. He appeared in four Challenge Cup finals, two for Warrington and two for St Helens. He won three England caps and also toured Australia in 1975 for the World Cup. He asked for a transfer early in the 1981-2 season and did not play for Fulham again.

Carl Radbone

Carl was a young Welsh Rugby Union player who joined Fulham from Penlan RUFC. He played as a centre or winger but could not win a regular place after making his debut in December 1980. He made 38 appearances for Fulham and left at the end of the 1982-3 season.

John Risman

Another recruit from a famous Rugby League family. John's father was Great Britain international Gus Risman and his brother Bev was an international in both Rugby codes and later Fulham's team manager. John was signed from Blackpool Borough, but had spent most of his career at Workington. He won three Welsh caps before joining Fulham. John mainly played at full back but could also play centre or on the wing. He left Fulham at the end of the first season to rejoin Blackpool Borough.

Peter Souto

Peter was Fulham's second recruit from Welsh Rugby Union. A strong second row forward, he joined Fulham from Cardiff RUFC and had also been a member of the Welsh international Rugby Union squad. He made his debut at home to Bramley in November 1980 and went on to make 71 appearances for the club before leaving at the end of the 1983-4 season. He then made a handful of appearances for Widnes and St Helens.

Neil Tuffs

Neil joined Fulham from Featherstone Rovers, the only other club he had played for in the professional game. He mainly played at centre and made 60 appearances for Fulham before joining another new club, the Maidstone based Kent Invicta, in the summer of 1983.

Ian van Bellen

Ian was the first Yorkshireman to sign for Fulham. He played in the pack, usually in the front row. Although signed as a squad player, he became the Fulham supporters' hero with his vast frame and balding head running into the opposition. He signed for Huddersfield as a 17 year old in 1963 and then played for Castleford and Bradford Northern, where he won First Division and Premiership honours. He was released at the end of Fulham's first season, much to his and the supporters' disappointment. He joined Blackpool and then played for Halifax, Kent Invicta and Keighley before retiring in 1985. By then he had played 21 seasons in the professional game.

John Wood

John was a powerfully built second row forward. He was signed by Fulham from Wigan and had previously played five seasons for Widnes, including a Challenge Cup final appearance in 1976. He played for Great Britain at under-24 level and for England in a match against France in Venice in 1982, which is not regarded as an official match in Rugby League's records. He left Fulham in 1983 to join Salford, but then retired due to injury.

Graham Worgan

Graham was signed from Leigh in October 1980 and played two games for Fulham at centre. He then returned to Leigh the next month.

Appendix 3: Player recruitment in Harold Genders's time at Fulham

Period covered July 1980 to October 1983

Player	Date signed	Left club
Roy Lester	July 1980	
Iain MacCorquodale	July 1980	July 1981 to Blackpool
Tony Karalius	July 1980	Retired May 1981. Joined Cardiff August 1981
Ian van Bellen	July 1980	July 1981 to Blackpool
John Risman	July 1980	July 1981 to Blackpool
Adrian Cambriani	July 1980	
Dave Allen	July 1980	
Reg Bowden	July 1980	
Derek Noonan	July 1980	Did not play after 1980-1981 season
David Hull	July 1980	Did not play 1981-1982 or 1982-1983, played 1983-1984
Tony Kinsey	July 1980	
Mal Aspey	August 1980	January 1982 to Wigan
John Wood	August 1980	June 1983 to Salford in exchange for Trevor Stockley
Tony Gourley	August 1980	
David Eckersley	August 1980	
Neil Tuffs	September 1980	June 1983 to Kent Invicta
Harry Beverley	September 1980	
Chris Ganley	October 1980	
Graham Worgan	October 1980	November 1980 back to Leigh
Peter Souto	November 1980	
Carl Radbone	December 1980	Left at end 1982-1983 season
Martin Herdman	December 1980	
Graham Moss	January 1981	Played 2 games on trial
Joe Doherty	March 1981	
Steve Diamond	May 1981	
John Dalgreen	May 1981	
John Crossley	August 1981	

Shaun Hoare	September 1981	
Hussain M'Barki	October 1981	
Harold Stringer	January 1982	Loan from Leigh until March 1982
Michael Walsh	February 1982	London amateur left end of 1981-1982
Chris Camilleri	March 1982	Loan from Barrow until April 1982
Frank Feighan	October 1982	London amateur trialist. Did not sign permanently.
Steve Bayliss	November 1982	
Steve Mills	March 1983	
Charlie Jones	March 1983	
Trevor Stockley	June 1983	
Alan Dearden	September 1983	

Some records show John O'Donovan and Gordon Walters joining the club in the summer of 1983, but in fact they never played for the club.

Some amateur players played for the club in 1981-1982 as trialists but did not sign permanently.

Appendix 4: The Bradford Northern Challenge Match

Printed below are the letter from Harold Genders to Bradford Northern confirming arrangements for the match and the press release issued by Fulham RLFC.

FULHAM RUGBY LEAGUE FOOTBALL CLUB LIMITED

CRAVEN COTTAGE, STEVENAGE ROAD, LONDON SW6 6HH
TELEPHONE 01-736 6561-3

25th March, 1981

Mr. J. Bates,
Chairman,
Bradford Northern
Odsal Stadium,
Bradford. R.L.F.C.,

Dear Jack & Fellow Directors,

Re: Match at Craven Cottage, Friday, 1st May, 1981
Kick-off 7.30 p.m.

I hereby confirm the following agreement for the above mentioned match.

1. Each team will provide their own insurance cover.
2. Both teams will be responsible for their own travelling

expenses to and from London, including accommodation.

3. Fulham R.L.F.C. will deduct from the gate receipts expenses such as gatemen, groundsmen, police etc. (these costs will be kept to a minimum) .

4. Every effort will be made to obtain a sponsor for the players wages on both sides for the full amount or part of them. If, however, we are unable to achieve this, the players monies will be deducted from the gate receipts and will be as follows:-

    a. The losing team will receive £800.00

    b. The winning team will receive £2,400

In the event of a draw, five minutes extra time will be played, and repeated, until a result is obtained.

The remainder of the gate will be divided between the two clubs as follows:-

    Fulham R.L.F.C. will receive 60%

    Bradford Northern R.L.F.C. will receive 40%

5. As discussed, we both have licence to abuse each other in the press in the interests of obtaining the maximum gate which will produce the best financial reward and the amount of money quoted in the press will not be adhered to.

I would like to thank you for the prompt and progressive way that you have agreed with us and I do hope we can both have a very financially rewarding and good night on the 1st May 1981.

Yours sincerely,

H.J. GENDERS
Managing Director

Fulham R.L.F.C. PRESS STATEMENT

It has been brought to my attention that the Bradford Northern Board of Directors have made a statement that Fulham R.L.F.C. will not hold their own in the First Division. Bradford Northern would do well to look at our record against First Division clubs this year. In the three encounters in Cup games, we beat Leeds 9-3, we only lost to Wakefield Trinity, who are currently second in the Rugby League table, by the narrow margin of 9-5 and it was also Wakefield who were hanging on in the second half when we were easily the better side. It must also be remembered that Leeds and Wakefield are two of the better clubs in Rugby League. It is also to be appreciated that with six matches left, we can lose two games and still be virtually certain of promotion to the First Division.

I am aware that Bradford Northern are the current Rugby League Champions and 1 therefore challenge the Chairman of the Club Jack Bates, through the press, to a rugby duel on the 1st May, 1981, the eve of the Rugby League Cup Final, at 7.30 p.m. at Craven Cottage and we put down £5,000 to prove we mean business and hope that Bradford Northern have the backbone to cover it. I would ask the Chairman to inform the press whether they are prepared to accept our challenge.

H. J. GENDERS

Appendix 5: 1980-1981 Attendances

Fulham had a major impact on the Second Division attendances. Overall, Second Division crowds increased from 302,345 in 1979-80 to 420,994 in 1980-81. This was an increase of 39.2%. The First and Second Divisions had an increase of over 175,000 supporters, which included the 85,337 who attended Fulham's home league matches. Including the Bradford Northern match, 123,456 people attended Fulham matches at Craven Cottage, an average of 7,262. Excluding the Bradford Northern match, the average was 7,058.

Fulham had the highest Second Division home average for league matches, 6,096. This was 1,403 ahead of the next highest, Wigan. This figure was also higher than all the First Division clubs except three, Hull, Hull KR and Bradford Northern. The latter's home average crowd was only 11 more than Fulham, and they had won the First Division championship.

In the John Player Trophy, the Fulham versus Leeds match had the highest attendance for the whole competition in 1980-81, except for the final. That final only attracted 237 more supporters than the Fulham game.

In British Rugby League overall that season, there were 36 gates of over 10,000. Of these, 24 were Hull FC matches. Of the other 12 matches, two involved Fulham. The Bradford Northern match is not included as it was not an official fixture.

On their travels, the club also attracted a great deal of interest, as the table below shows. Eight clubs had their highest gate for Fulham's visit, and for another three clubs Fulham drew their second highest gate of the season. Wigan were playing their first ever season in the Second Division and were also an attraction as visitors, particularly for clashes with other Lancashire teams. Only three crowds of less than 1,000 watched Fulham matches.

Opponents	Average home attendance	Fulham match	Highest Gate of season	% above average (League Matches)	Notes
Batley	1,329	3,250	Yes	145%	1.
Rochdale	1,149	2,750	Yes	139%	
Hunslet	931	1,842	Yes	98%	
York	3,827	7,351	Yes	92%	
Keighley	1,612	3,027	Yes	87%	
Huyton	270	500	Second highest	85%	
Swinton	1,935	3,550	Yes	83%	
Dewsbury	1,377	2,500	Yes	82%	
Wigan	4,693	8,100	Yes	72%	
Bramley	1,050	1,750	Second highest	67%	
Whitehaven	2,733	4,235	Second highest	55%	
Huddersfield	1,769	2,435	Third highest	38%	
Blackpool	684	906	Third highest	32%	
Doncaster	628	672	Fourth highest	7%	2.
Total	23,977	39,618			
Average	1,712	2,830		65%	
Fulham home matches	6,096				

Notes:
Different sources give different figures for attendances. The above are from the Fulham RLFC match programme.
1. This was Batley's centenary match
2. Doncaster's home gates were between 296 and 779 except for the visit of York at the end of the season which attracted 3,000 people.

Appendix 6: 1980-1981 Statistics and records

Results   1980-1981

Home matches in **bold**

Wigan	**D2**	**14.9.80**	**24-5**	**9,554**
Keighley	D2	21.9.80	13-24	3,027
Swinton	**D2**	**28.9.80**	**25-11**	**5,589**
Blackpool	D2	5.10.80	15-2	906
Huddersfield	**D2**	**12.10.80**	**30-7**	**5,971**
Doncaster	D2	19.10.80	28-16	672
York	**D2**	**26.10.80**	**23-5**	**7,159**
Bramley	**D2**	**9.11.80**	**10-7**	**5,405**
Dewsbury	D2	16.11.80	9-7	2,500
Leeds	**JPT1**	**23.11.80**	**9-3**	**12,583**
Wigan	D2	30.11.80	2-15	8,100
Leigh	JPT2	7.12.80	9-17	7,606
Hunslet	**D2**	**21.12.80**	**19-5**	**5,629**
Batley	**D2**	**28.12.80**	**15-5**	**6,237**
Whitehaven	D2	4.1.81	0-6	4,235
Rochdale	**D2**	**11.1.81**	**8-24**	**6,162**
Bramley	D2	18.1.81	21-11	1,750
Huyton	**D2**	**25.1.81**	**25-4**	**5,805**
Hunslet	D2	1.2.81	12-11	1,842
Swinton	D2	8.2.81	9-13	3,550
Wakefield T	**CC 1**	**15.2.81**	**5-9**	**15,013**
Blackpool	**D2**	**1.3.81**	**8-0**	**4,715**
Keighley	**D2**	**8.3.81**	**24-3**	**5,285**
Huyton	D2	15.3.81	19-3	500
Dewsbury	**D2**	**22.3.81**	**16-4**	**5,258**
York	D2	29.3.81	10-15	7,351
Whitehaven	**D2**	**5.4.81**	**15-0**	**6,707**
Batley	D2	12.4.81	8-10	3,250
Rochdale	D2	16.4.81	19-5	2,750
Huddersfield	D2	19.4.81	3-8	2,435
Doncaster	**D2**	**20.4.81**	**37-11**	**5,867**
Bradford	**Challenge**	**1.5.81**	**20-8**	**11,926**

Player appearances 1980-1981

	A	S	TA	T	G	DG	Pts
Dave Allen	23	2	25	4	0	0	12
Mal Aspey	23	4	27	16	0	0	48
Harry Beverley	22	0	22	2	0	0	6
Reg Bowden	28	1	29	4	0	0	12
Adrian Cambriani	26	0	26	13	0	0	39
Joe Doherty	5	1	6	0	0	0	0
David Eckersley	25	2	27	12	5	10	56
Chris Ganley	19	0	19	8	0	0	24
Tony Gourley	21	3	24	1	0	0	3
Martin Herdman	7	6	13	2	0	0	6
David Hull	25	1	26	2	0	0	6
Tony Karalius	20	2	22	2	0	0	6
Roy Lester	15	8	23	3	0	0	9
Iain MacCorquodale	28	0	28	6	75	3	171
Graham Moss	2	0	2	0	0	0	0
Derek Noonan	18	0	18	4	0	0	12
Carl Radbone	9	0	9	2	3	0	12
John Risman	18	4	22	3	0	0	9
Peter Souto	4	7	11	1	0	0	3
Neil Tuffs	7	7	14	3	0	0	9
Ian van Bellen	20	3	23	4	0	0	12
John Wood	23	2	25	4	0	0	12
Graham Worgan	2	0	2	0	0	0	0

Key:
A: Appearances S: Substitute TA: Total appearances
T: Tries G: Goals D: Drop-goals
Pts: Points

Appearances in league and cup matches only are included in this table.

The 1980-1981 Second Division final league table

	Pl PTS	W	D	L	Pts f	Pts a	
York	28	23	0	5	649	331	46
Wigan	28	20	3	5	597	293	43
Fulham	**28**	**20**	**0**	**8**	**447**	**237**	**40**
Whitehaven	28	19	1	8	409	250	39
Huddersfield	28	18	1	9	429	310	37
Swinton	28	17	2	9	440	302	36
Keighley	28	14	1	13	445	501	29
Hunslet	28	13	1	14	447	430	27
Bramley	28	13	1	14	433	431	27
Rochdale H	28	13	0	15	406	418	26
Batley	28	12	0	16	328	405	24
Dewsbury	28	11	1	16	346	364	23
Doncaster	28	5	0	23	250	562	10
Blackpool B	28	4	1	23	212	419	9
Huyton	28	2	0	26	211	796	4

The top four teams were promoted to the First Division.

Key:
Pl: Played
W: Won
D: Drawn
L: Lost
Pts f: Points scored for
Pts a: Points scored against
PTS: League points

Appendix 7: 1980-1981 Honours and awards

The team finished third in the Second Division and were promoted.

International caps:
Adrian Cambriani: 2 caps versus France and England
Martin Herdman: 1 cap versus England

Open Rugby **magazine:**
Team of the year
Coach of the year: Reg Bowden
Best programme of the year

Seerena Coach of the month:
October 1980: Reg Bowden

Daily Mirror - **Shopacheck Team of the Month:**
October 1980: Fulham

Greenall Whitley - *Sunday People***:**
Personality of the year: Reg Bowden

Trumanns Man of Steel:
Coach of the Year: Reg Bowden was one of two runners up.

Index

This index only covers chapters 1-12, not the appendices.

Books from London League Publications

From Fulham to Wembley
20 years of Rugby League in London

Edited by Peter Lush and Dave Farrar

A celebration of 20 years of professional Rugby League in the capital. Includes profiles of the key players and coaches, major match reports and memories and recollections of people involved with the club.
The Independent's "Sports Book of the Week" June 2000

Published in June 2000 at £8.75. special offer to readers of this book: £8.00.

Touch and Go
A history of professional Rugby League in London

By Dave Farrar and Peter Lush with Michael O'Hare

Covers the international matches played in London, the first Wembley Challenge Cup Final and a full history of all the professional club sides in London from the 1930s to 1995.
Published in 1995 at £9.00. Special offer to clear last few copies £5.00.

Tries in the Valleys
A history of Rugby League in Wales

Edited by Peter Lush and Dave Farrar

Includes a history of the Welsh Rugby League team and all the club sides that have played in Wales. Many interviews and a comprehensive statistics section.
Published in 1998 at £14.95. Special offer £8.00.

Going to the Cricket
A guide to British first class cricket grounds

By Robin Osmond and Peter David Lush
Published in 1999 at £5.95. Special offer £5.00

From Arundel to Zimbabwe
A cricket followers guide to British and international cricket
grounds

By Robin Osmond, Peter David Lush and Dave Farrar
Published in 1997 at £6.50. Special offer £3.00

Boxing Shadows
1500 Boxing Quiz questions

by Ralph Oates
Published in 1997 at £6.95. Special offer £2.50

Have you got the Bottle?
A basic guide to bottle collecting and digging

By John Woodhams
Published in 1998 at £9.95. Special offer £9.00

All books post free

Order from: London League Publications Ltd
                P.O. Box 10441
                London E14 0SB

Please make cheques payable to London League Publications Ltd.
No credit card orders.

Further information from: 020-7515-2001.